Life
MAGIC

THE POWER OF POSITIVE WITCHCRAFT

Life
MAGIC

THE POWER OF POSITIVE WITCHCRAFT

 Susan BOWES

SIMON&
SCHUSTER
EDITIONS

SIMON & SCHUSTER EDITIONS
Rockefeller Center
1230 Avenue of the Americas
New York, New York 10020

Text by Susan Bowes

1 3 5 7 9 10 8 6 4 2

Library of Congress Cataloging-in-Publication Data is available.

ISBN 0-684-85354-X

This book was conceived, designed, and produced by
THE IVY PRESS LIMITED
2/3 St. Andrews Place
Lewes, East Sussex
BN7 1UP

EDITORIAL DIRECTOR *Sophie Collins*
ART DIRECTOR *Peter Bridgewater*
DESIGNER AND PAGE LAYOUT *Sara Nunan*
PROJECT EDITOR *Nicola Young*
COMMISSIONING EDITOR *Viv Croot*
ILLUSTRATIONS *Kim Glass, Sarah Young*
PICTURE RESEARCH *Lynda Marshall*

Printed and bound in Singapore

Dedicated to: Makemake the Great Bird Creator, God of Easter Island
and Demeter, Goddess of the Land

Other Books by Susan Bowes:
Notions and Potions
Love Spells and Rituals

Half-Title Page: ABUNDANCE AND THE FOUR ELEMENTS (DETAIL)
Jan Brueghel

Title Page: NYMPHS FINDING THE HEAD OF ORPHEUS
John William Waterhouse

❬ The Birth of Venus *(Sandro Botticelli, detail).* ❭

CONTENTS

INTRODUCTION

Life Magic is a celebration of the Goddess and the Old Crafts—those magical and mysterious ways that most of us have forgotten. Modern hedonistic pursuits leave little room for the enchanted sorcery of life, and the romance of the unknown finds little comfort among the audio and visual aids that assail our senses from morning to night. But rest assured, the ways of the Goddess are there in every puff of wind, ripple of water, crackle of fire, and clod of soil. The Goddess, mistress of the hidden traditions, speaks to us in our dreamtime and in those silent moments when suddenly everything comes clear. She brings us those challenges and people we need to meet in order for our path to unfold, and in a blink of an eye takes away things that no longer serve. She is the nurturing mother as well as the hag of destruction. Nature is her embodiment on Earth, just as the moon is her totality in the heavens. She is

Day and Night (*Edward Robert Hughes, detail*). *The Goddess is with us at every moment, in all of nature. She visits us in our dreams and shows the way ahead.*

Phaeton Sunrise (*Sir William Blake Richmond, detail*). *Where light meets dark, creation begins.*

the universal female principle, consort to her lord God, the male principle. Together they bring the very essence of life into being through the unification of the light and the dark, the positive and negative, the manifest and unmanifest and, of course, man and woman. The Goddess represents the power of the divine female, the ancient goddess principle that rests at the heart of all the old religions. She bathes in her own magnificence; she evokes and harnesses the very creative force of life itself.

Yet because of the influence of the patriarchal Christian religion over the last two thousand years, the Goddess is regarded with suspicion in Western eyes. To many she is the enchantress, the temptress, the path to lunacy and ruin.

But how can there be balance and harmony without the female principle? Indeed, how can life perpetuate itself in her absence? It is simply impossible, just as it is impossible for the spark of life to be created without the gift of the male principle. Everything in the natural world holds the masculine and feminine elements at its core; one cannot survive without the other. The famous Yin/Yang symbol of the ancient Taoist teachings

Positive and negative, feminine and masculine—one cannot exist without the other. The ancient Chinese Yin/Yang symbol (bottom right) represents life's essential balance and harmony. As we return to the principle of the Goddess we remember eternal, forgotten truths…

Radiant Moon (*Edward Robert Hughes, detail*).
*The moon features strongly in our emotions and
energies. Spiritual reawakening begins when we allow
ourselves to be guided by the natural law.*

shows these two forces intertwining in perfect unity, and this unity is expressed through the many different cycles, rhythms, and patterns found throughout the universe, right down to the molecular makeup of our own cell structure. The God and Goddess express the universal consciousness, the higher forces that govern every facet of life on Earth and they are an intrinsic part of us.

Today, there seems to be a spiritual reawakening. Many important questions have been left unanswered by the major religions. Disillusioned people are seeking other forms of spiritual guidance, and many are returning to the Old Ways to find a sense of purpose in their lives. At the same time, many people realize that the survival of the planet calls for a more compassionate regard for nature, as embodied in the symbolism of the Goddess. Her divine power is once more beginning to be acknowledged and realized.

In tribute to the triple vision of the Goddess (maiden, mother, and crone) *Life Magic* has been divided into three sections:

1. The Return of the Goddess
2. Symbolism and the Old Crafts
3. Spells, Rituals, and Ceremonies.

To those who remain skeptical about the Old Ways, I hope *Life Magic* will help to dispel their concerns and demystify the ancient Craft of the Wise. These crafts are not bizarre practices or the ramblings of a few eccentrics; they are beautiful, gentle rituals incorporating the glory of nature with time-honored mystic symbolism that humankind has developed since the dawn of time in the search for the truth. To those who wish to know more, I trust this book will also provide plenty of practical advice on how to enhance your ritual work. Above all, this book is a celebration of the Goddess—a reminder of how she was revered in ancient time, and how we need to incorporate her into our contemporary lifestyles to attain the peace and harmony we all seek in both our inner and outer worlds.

Now is the Pilgrim Year Fair Autumn's Charge
(*John Byam Liston Shaw, detail*). *In working with
nature, we harness the gentle powers of the Goddess.*

Part One

THE RETURN
OF THE GODDESS

CHAPTER 1

THE GOD AND GODDESS

THE MALE AND FEMALE PRINCIPLE

The God and the Goddess are the divine aspects of the male and female principle and the essence of all life. In antiquity, people lived closer to nature, and their gods and goddesses were instinctively associated with the natural elements. Throughout many cultures the symbol of the Goddess is the Earth and the moon, while her consort is the sky and the sun. She is dark mystery; he is fiery energy. When the two meet, creation occurs. Because the Goddess is the embodiment of the Earth, she is equated with the mother, the nurturer, and the provider. Ancient civilizations built temples and shrines in homage to her might and power, and great celebrations and festivals were held in her honor. She was the ultimate focus for all religious worship throughout the ancient world, for without the protection of the bountiful divine mother, famine would sweep across the land. As the great provider, she was intrinsically bound up with the destiny of humankind. Another great blessing from the divine forces was sexual passion since it ensured the continuation of life. Sexuality and religion were inherently linked in the minds of the ancients. To enter into an act that appeased and pleased both mortal and immortal beings was considered the highest form of devotion.

THE GODDESS IN BABYLONIAN, GREEK, AND ROMAN MYTHOLOGY

Over three thousand years ago in Babylon, the Goddess was revered as Astarte or Ishtar. Her temple priestesses would conduct powerful fertility rituals with chosen consorts to ensure the continuing fecundity of the land. These sexual acts performed by the priestesses were considered sacred. They were honored as the most divine embodiment of the Goddess, those

The Goddess Hathor Placing the Magic Collar on Seti I
(*Ancient Egyptian, painted limestone relief, Valley of the Kings*). *Ancient cultures understood the vital interaction of the male and female elements.*

Diana with her Bow and Arrow (*Roman fresco*). *In the ancient world, the Goddess was acknowledged as humankind's great protector and provider. Temples and shrines were built in her honor.*

who could excite the sacred communion between the body and soul. In this respect they bore the original title of virgin, meaning maiden or unmarried rather than a person who had never experienced sexual union.

It is said that in ancient Babylonian times young girls, before entering marriage, were initiated into womanhood within the sanctity of the temple. They were compelled to give themselves to the first stranger who threw money into their laps. This fee was then given to the temple as an offering. However, since both parties entered into their union in full knowledge that they were being

Goddess, and their role was to act as ritual "brides" to the king who became the embodiment of the divine God. This blessed union ensured the prowess of the king and, therefore, his suitability to symbolize the fertility of the land.

In ancient Rome, six virgins, usually aged between six and ten, were specially

Bacchante Dancing
*(detail from Roman fresco,
Pompeii). Music and dance
played a vital part in
ancient rituals.*

selected from highly influential families to serve Vesta, the Roman Goddess of Hearth and Home. By tending to the sacred fire of the Goddess, these vestal virgins ensured that the heart of the city would burn as brightly as the Goddess's fire. Vestal virgins were meant to be chaste during their 30 years of service, and any found straying from the path of celibacy were walled up alive in punishment. It is possible, however, that some entered into secret sexual initiation ceremonies with the high priest.

Women Performing the Cult Of Eleusinian Mystery *(Roman fresco, Pompeii). The city's vital spark was ensured by tending the sacred fire of Vesta, Goddess of Hearth and Home.*

blessed by the Goddess, this sacrifice of innocent purity was regarded with great reverence and honor. Most young women would then return home in preparation for marriage or a life of chastity. But some women chose to spend their entire lives in service to the temple and the

The Greeks and Romans had many names for the Goddess, each one symbolizing a vital part of the female psyche, from the gentle to the terrible. The Greek goddess Hecate, for example, has some particularly cruel attributes. Accompanied by her howling dogs, she is queen of the underworld, the destroyer who haunts tombs and crossroads, and woe betide anyone who crosses her. Hecate is also part of the threefold vision of the moon, the root of all magic.

THE GODDESS ISIS

Perhaps the most famous name for the Goddess is Isis. She was the mythological Egyptian queen who ruled her people with such fairness and devotion that they constructed enormous temples in her honor. The Greeks identified her with Athene and Demeter, and later her worship spread throughout the Greek and Roman worlds. She was married to her

brother Osiris who was murdered by his jealous brother Set. Set had Osiris' body cut into 15 pieces and scattered far and wide; however, Isis used her imperial magic powers to locate the pieces and impregnated herself with the thirteenth piece, his dismembered phallus. Osiris metamorphosed into the constellation of Orion and Ruler of the Dead and Dying, and Isis gave birth to Horus, who was destined to become the all-powerful sky god and falcon god, and prince to his people. When he reached manhood, Horus wreaked revenge on Set, destroying him. Horus then became the first pharaoh of Egypt and the eternal eye of Ra—the mighty sun god who ruled supreme over the multitude of Egyptian gods and goddesses

The legendary Egyptian Goddess Isis commanded great respect from her people, who built many temples in her honor. She symbolizes the spirit of fertility and generosity.

The Departed Before Osiris, Isis, and Thoth (Egyptian tomb painting). Such was the power of belief in the gods and the afterlife, the ancient dynasty thrived for 3,000 years.

Artemis, Goddess of Hunting, symbolizes the maiden or virgin new moon; Demeter, Goddess of the Earth, represents the mother or full moon; and Hecate corresponds to the hag or dark moon. Each of these facets reveals the three states of woman: the maiden who is full of waiting potential; the mother who is realized potential; and the hag who is wasted or destroyed potential. The moon is queen of the night, and the womb to which we all return to rest and sleep. She is also mistress of our dreams and therefore witness to our deepest secrets. She is ruler of our emotions just as she controls the ebb and flow of the oceans' tides and all the cycles of nature.

THE GODDESS IN
HINDU PHILOSOPHY

Hindu philosophy also embraces the higher sexual aspects of the God and Goddess. This manifests through Vishnu and his consort Lakshmi. Vishnu, according to the Vedas—the ancient Hindu text—helped to create the universe when he took three steps through the cosmos to give form to the earth, the air, and the heavens. Lakshmi and Vishnu are usually depicted together resting on a bed made from the coils of Ananta, the cosmic snake who protects them by fanning out his many heads as he floats on the waters of eternity. The serpent energy is directly linked with the kundalini energy, the vital creative sexual force that unifies humankind with the gods.

It is said that from time to time when humanity is facing a period of crisis, Vishnu incarnates into the world he created as an avatar—an embodiment of the divine principle. Since he has

The God Vishnu Resting on a Snake (Indian wall painting). The energy of the cosmic snake symbolizes the creative sexual force that links us with the gods.

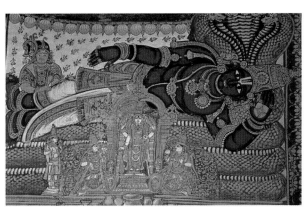

returned to the world he created, he automatically attracts great controversy. Many claim that the Bhagwan Shree Rajneesh, named Osho after his death, was indeed Vishnu. His name Rajneesh means Lord of the Full Moon. There is little doubt that he died by foul means because his controversial political and religious teachings were regarded by some as highly contentious and threatening.

Shakti sitting on a Throne (Indian wall painting). Shakti embodies a combination of the Ying and Yang.

In Hindu philosophy, sacred duality is also symbolized by the god and goddess, Shiva and Shakti. Shakti contains the Yin and Yang principles, the pulsation of creation that gives form. These two complementary polarities give rise to the innate differences between man and woman. Shakti represents the state of becoming or potential. In total contrast, Shiva, her consort, is beyond form. He symbolizes pure being, a never-changing "isness," a transcendental state beyond everything. The symbolism of Shakti and Shiva illustrates that the male principle cannot manifest on its own. It must enter through the female principle in order for the life force to become a reality. Many say that the Indian guru, Sai Baba, is the current physical embodiment of Shakti and Shiva. Certainly he is capable of magical manifestations, and his sacred healing ash, or vibhuti, can be found pouring from his photographs.

THE GODDESS IN PAGAN MYTHOLOGIES

In prehistoric societies, the Great Earth Mother Goddess was always depicted with wide childbearing hips and large sensuous breasts. She was the embodiment of fertility, the vessel for the continuation of life. When a hunter returned victorious from his kill, he would wear the horns of his prey as a mark of his prowess and couple with a specially chosen fertile woman. He represented the Horned God and she represented the Earth Mother. It was believed that through this powerful union their child would be imbued

Eve (Turkish miniature).
The sensuous figure of Eve embodied the celebration of life and sexuality in pre-Christian times.

with extraordinary qualities, which would increase its ability to survive and thrive, and enhance the entire tribe. This sexual union was also regarded as a tribute to the animal that had sacrificed its life for the well-being of the tribe. They thought the animal could return in human form, and this belief is the possible origin of the mythical creatures that were half-man/half-beast.

The celebrated union between the Horned God and the Earth Mother would have occurred mainly during spring and autumn. The first hunt would provide food for the tribe after the long winter months, while the second was the opportunity to stock up before the cold spell began. It also ensured that most babies would be born early in the year or over the ensuing summer months, having been protected from the harshness of the winter in a warm womb.

The Horned God was found in almost every ancient culture. In fact, Karnak, the great temple in Egypt, was dedicated to the horned god Ammon-Ra. In many civilizations, sacred places were depicted by horns. Even the Old Testament is dotted with references to horns, for instance, the "horns of the altar" and "the horn of my salvation." Conquering nations placed horns on their helmets to symbolize their prowess, and some Native American cultures continue to use the horn as part of their ceremonial dress. The Horned God is Lord of Virility, the Master of Spring. This is why the ancients chose the astrological symbol of Aries, the horned ram, to mark the spring equinox on March 21, when the earth quickens for rebirth.

With the advent of Christianity, the Horned God was transformed into the Devil, in an attempt to discredit the ancient sexual empowerment rituals. In doing so, the Christian

Church was able to undermine the very basis of the old religions. Sex became a base performance, fit for beasts. So the old ways were killed, mutilated, and ridiculed, and women were equated with Eve, the wicked temptress whose actions single-handedly banished humanity from the Garden of Eden.

Yet it is impossible to banish sexual desire—it is the root of all creation and to suppress it results in guilt, perversion, and fear. The power

A Diablerie (*Cornelis Saftleven*).
The suppression by established religions of the natural flow and celebration of sexuality has led to perverse and destructive ways that reverberate throughout the planet.

of woman was almost obliterated, and thus was the true power of man diminished. What were left were empty human husks, devoid of the natural flow of sexuality that brings sustaining contact with the Earth Mother. This has had appalling repercussions. Men and women have lost respect for themselves, resulting in a devastating loss of respect for the land itself. Destruction and abuse have replaced honor and devotion.

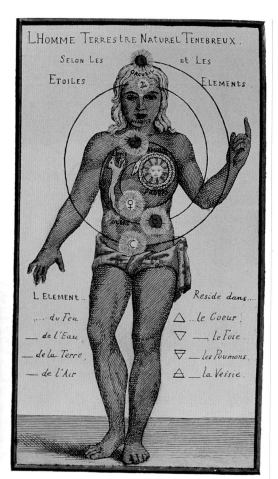

The Cosmic Spiral Within the Body of Man
(from J.G. Gritchel's Theosophica Practica, *showing chakras or centers of psychic energy). "Going with the flow" of our own intuition will unblock energy channels.*

THE RETURN OF THE GODDESS

As the modern world seems beset with insurmountable problems, people are beginning to look to the old mythology of the Goddess to find their own alternative and innovative solutions. For this reason, the Goddess must be allowed to live again in our own times, and people need to experience their inner pride as they take her back into their lives. The Goddess is the divine inspiration for humanity. She is not only Queen of the Heavens and Earth, she is also Goddess of Sexual Love. It is through union with her that humanity can return to its highest spiritual glory. However, the union must be an act of selfless devotion on the highest level if its most fruitful aspects are to be achieved.

According to all the ancient texts and scriptures, humans are indeed made in the image of God. This means that every woman on this earth is the embodiment of the female principle and every man is the embodiment of the male principle. It is time for a mutual acknowledgment of one another's power and glory. This cannot be accomplished in a spirit of competition or of rivalry. It requires instead a mutual respect based on our natural need for one another, a need that only an opposite entity can meet and satisfy.

The creatures that share our world have not
forgotten their own affinity with the natural
order. Animals have always figured strongly in
ancient beliefs and customs and, more than ever
today, have much to teach us about living in
harmony with the environment.

CHAPTER 2

TOTEM ANIMALS

Animals are very important to the Goddess because they act as her link or bridge between the seen and unseen worlds. Since ancient times animals have fulfilled this role; tribes-people would wear the bones, teeth, and skins of animals as power totems or as protective amulets and charms.

The art of hunting was as sacred as any other ritual ceremony. Before the hunt commenced, the entire village would enter into a religious dance to bless the hunters and the hunted. The officiating priest and priestess would make contact with the spirit of the animal that was to die for the benefit of the people before granting permission for the hunt to begin. Great honor was heaped upon the animal, for without its ultimate sacrifice of life there would be no food. Every part of the animal was used in some way—its meat for food; its skin for clothes, shoes, and floor covering; its sinews for ropes and binding; its bones and teeth for cooking and work utensils and personal charms.

Certain animals are very closely associated with the Goddess and witchcraft. These "little helpers" were traditionally known as familiars. During the

Siamese Cats (*Jacques Nam*).
Cat lovers value the mystical quality of their pets, while others regard it with superstition. Cats have always been regarded as a link with the spiritual world.

witch hunts of the Middle Ages, familiars were considered to be demon spirits in disguise. As a result, many were destroyed or burnt in the fire with their owners.

Animal magic is powerful. It is said that any animal that crosses your path has been sent with a profound message by the Goddess. Take note of any animal you see on your travels. Call out to its spirit and see what answer you receive.

THE CAT

The most famous familiar is of course the cat, especially the black cat. It is thought to be in close contact with the spirits and to act as a crossover between the two worlds. The domestic cat originated in ancient Egypt where it was regarded as highly sacred, carrying the spirit of Isis herself. Egypt had a very powerful cat culture centered around the cat goddess Bast. Many excavated tombs contained the remains of mummified cats and sarcophagi crafted in the shapes of cats.

The sensuous and rapacious cat, who can change in an instant into a spiteful fury, demanding attention only on its own terms, is said to be the personification of woman!

Twilight *(William J. Webb). Animals, birds, and insects continue to live in the natural, psychic dimension which has come to be disregarded by much of humankind in this "progressive" age.*

The Goat Girl (*Edith Ridley Corbet*).
In pagan times, the horned goat symbolized the male God, consort of the Goddess.

The word "pussy" refers to the vulva of the Goddess; therefore, the "puss cat" is associated with fertility. The cat is very much a creature of the moon; its nocturnal habits are shrouded in mystery, and even the most cynical owner swears their charge has very partic- ular powers. Many people today are still wary of crossing the path of a black cat; this belief stems from the Middle Ages when it was said that witches rode abroad disguised as black cats in order to perform their nefarious deeds.

THE GOAT

Just as the cat symbolizes the Goddess, the goat symbolizes the God. The most famous goat-god is Pan, the Horned One. *Pan* is a Greek word meaning "all" or "everything," and Pan personifies all that exists, the life force of the world. He is always depicted playing a seven- reed pipe. Seven is the sacred occult number symbolizing life itself because it contains the four elements of the body—spirit, flesh, bone, and humors—and the three elements of the soul— passion, desire, and reason. Seven also represents the ancient number of cosmic order: seven days in creation, seven days of the week, seven years of completion, seven wonders of the world, the seven chakras, the seven notes of the musical scale

Hares in a Wiltshire Landscape *(David Inshaw). The joyful dancing of the March hare was symbolic of virility and rebirth. Hares had a sacred link with Eostre, Goddess of Spring.*

and heavenly harmonies. Pan leads the dance of delight, and encourages his followers to celebrate the sensuality of life. However, the Christian Church, in its attempt to discredit these ancient customs, associated the Horned God and Pan with the Devil, and the goat was demoted to an animal of ridicule.

THE HARE

The hare is another creature sacred to the Goddess. It represents the corn spirit and the two equinoxes and is therefore associated with rebirth, fertility, and abun- dance. It is considered a powerful shape-shifter because it lives in shallow hollows on open land that are difficult to find. When caught off-guard, a hare will make a dash for safety, criss- crossing over the field in a very strange and alarming manner. Hares often sit in a ring, which was considered akin to the witches' sabbat; in Christian times this earned hares the reputa- tion of demons in disguise. In the pre-Christian era, the hare symbolized the virility of spring and was closely associated with the goddess Eostre, the Saxon goddess of spring. When the Christian Church transformed this old pagan festival in honor of Eostre into their celebration of the risen Christ at Easter, the hare was debased into the Easter bunny.

THE TOAD

The toad, in the idiom of the fairy tale, is the handsome prince in disguise. It represents hidden beauty, sensitivity, and power. Because it is amphibious—living half in and half out of water—it is very much associated with the undines, the water spirits, who, it is said, take care of the toad's spawn. And since the ponds, lakes, and streams where the toad lives are fed from underground springs, the toad is representative of the hidden world and deep truths. Toads exude a milky substance, known as toad's milk, from their skin when frightened or excited. Though this is extremely poisonous, it is believed to contain certain magical qualities that have been used by witches for hundreds of years. They love to eat insects and can be found hopping around in country gardens in pursuit

The snake symbolizes the kundalini, *or sexual energy. It also represents transmutation—as the snake sheds its skin, so we can choose to cast off our own outmoded thinking.*

of such delicacies and, of course, croaking a warning of danger to their human companions. The toad can reputedly bring rain and purification and is therefore a must as a familiar for anyone who works with the Old Crafts.

THE SNAKE

Since the beginning of time, the snake has represented sexual and creative forces. "If you take hold of a serpent too tightly it will bite you, too loose and you will lose it. The test of serpent power is to find the correct balance and keep it." This ancient occult teaching is the key to our inner source and power—the *kundalini*, or sexual energy. This vital life force dwells in the base of our spine, and to come to terms with it is perhaps the greatest test of all.

Serpent worship was practiced in many early civilizations. They regarded the snake as a holy and divine creature, capable of entering the underworld at will to receive messages from the dead. It was a symbol of transformation since it was able to shed an old skin to reveal a new one. In alchemy, the serpent's head represents the alpha and its tail the omega—the beginning and the end. The famous symbol of the snake swallowing its own tail is the sign of eternity and immortality. Two serpents entwined on a vertical staff—the emblem of the healing fraternity—represent the vital elements of Yin and Yang and the ability to transmute negative programing into positive self-healing. This is symbolized by shedding the old skin for the new. As we heal ourselves we become reborn, concentrating on the positive and leaving the old life behind.

*The raven was believed to be the messenger of
enlightenment. Light cannot exist without
darkness—by facing the dark void
we can find the light.*

THE RAVEN

All birds are regarded as messengers; but it is the raven that carries the magic. Its blue-black iridescent plumage symbolizes dark mystery, the void into which we must look if we are to find the light. It is also the guardian of ceremonial magic and absent healing: when thoughts of healing are sent to those in need, the raven acts as courier. It is also a bird of protection. It is said that the ravens that roost in the Tower of London are the reason for Britain's continuing peace. They guard the spirit of Bran the Blessed, a mighty god whose noble head is thought to lie buried under the Tower to protect the land against invasion. When the ravens leave, disaster and destruction will surely follow because Bran's spirit has also departed. In Norse mythology, two ravens, Hugin and Munin, gave the gift of wisdom and knowledge to the god Odin.

THE WHITE HORSE

The white horse is the Goddess's most powerful totem animal. It symbolizes power and purity, courage, speed, and strength. This symbol can be found depicted throughout the British Isles, cut into hillsides that are sacred sites for Goddess worship. The horse is dedicated to Rhiannon, the Welsh goddess of abundance and fertility.

A Gray Arab Stallion in a Wooded Landscape *(Jacques-Laurent Agasse). The beauty, sensitivity,
and strength of the white horse are the qualities most powerfully symbolic of the eternal Goddess.*

CHAPTER 3

LUNAR MAGIC

Scenes of Australia (*Joseph Lycett, detail*). *The movements of the moon affect us physically, emotionally, and spiritually.*

The moon is fundamental to any ritual work. It is the essence of mystery, magic, and mayhem. We all know the strange effect the full moon can have upon the behavior of both animals and humans. It is from this peculiar conduct that the word "lunacy" originates, and it is a known fact that violence and emotional problems always accelerate around the time of the full moon. It is easy to see why.

The moon governs the ebb and flow of all the water on Earth through its gravitational pull. During full-moon phases, when the sun and moon are in alignment with the Earth, there is a particularly strong gravitational pull on the ocean's surface, creating what is known as a high spring tide. Since the human body consists of over 70 percent water and emotions are strongly affected by the watery elements, this gravitational pull also influences our behavior. This phenomenon is echoed throughout the natural world, which is why it is most important to select herbs for magical work during the full moon when their water content and potency are at their height.

In early times, great importance was given to the phases of the moon for farming activities. It was considered fortuitous to plant seeds during the waxing phase of the moon when the water content of the soil was building. Animals born during this phase appeared to be more robust, and certainly juicier to eat when slaughtered before the full moon. Fishermen had greater success when clamming, shrimping, and crabbing in this period. Leaving castration of herd animals and the removal of their horns until the waning phase of the moon meant there was much less bleeding.

The ancients measured the passing of the seasons by the movement of the moon, the sun, and the stars. In fact, the word "moon" originates from the Sanskrit root *me*, meaning measure. "Month" is also a derivative of "moon."

"Lunar herbs." The gravitational pull of the full moon ensures the greatest magical potency of herbs gathered at this time for ritual purposes.

Luna *(Evelyn de Morgan). Many people are affected by the full moon. By understanding the different phases we can use their mystical power to enhance magical rituals.*

On the Trees, near Barnard Castle (*John Atkinson Grimshaw*). *The moon is the Goddess of the Night, mistress of our dreams and emotions and witness to our deepest secrets.*

THE THIRTEENTH MONTH OF THE LUNAR CALENDAR

The ancient Celtic calendar was accurately based on 13 lunar months. The moon orbits the Earth approximately every twenty-nine and a half days, but the sun signs are on average about a day longer than the lunar month. Consequently, each new moon starts earlier in a sun-sign period, until a new moon occurs so soon after the start of the sun sign that there is room for the entire lunar month before the sun sign changes. Two new moons appear in the same sun sign every two to three years. When this happens, adjustments are made by adding the thirteenth lunar month, which is allowed to fall where it will. Since the sun-sign periods are slightly longer in the summer, two new moons occur more often during the summer months than during the winter months. The moon for this thirteenth month is referred to as the Blue Moon; a mysterious changeable moon full of magical powers.

A number of ancient traditions incorporate the thirteenth month into their lunar calendars. The Jewish calendar, for instance, adds a second month of Adar when required. The Hindu and Chinese lunar calendars also add an extra month during the year when two lunar months start in the same sun sign. The Buddhists revere the power of the full moon in Taurus and Gemini because they believe that these two full moons open the door to the higher consciousness. They have a celebration on the full moon during the time of Taurus and Gemini called the Wesak festival. This ties in with Egyptian mythology; Isis, Goddess of the Moon and mistress of mystical knowledge, is associated with Taurus. The missing thirteenth astrological sign—known as Arachne, the spider, who spins the web of life—is said to have fallen between Taurus and Gemini.

It should be noted that there are some lunar calendars that neatly fit the 13 full moons into a fixed circle akin to astrological sun signs. There is nothing wrong with this for convenience, but remember that the moon is nebulous and changeable—just like the Goddess herself—so each year the true lengths of the months vary according to the dates of the new moon. If you

The Fine Flower of Histories Map of the Universe (Turkish manuscript). The "Blue Moon" of the thirteenth month was considered particularly auspicious and is still recognized by some traditions today.

Qui expanfis in cruce manibu
traxifti omnia ad te SECVLA

In principio erat
verbum.

The Tree of Life (*Gospel of St. John, sixteenth-century*). *The Tree of Life, with its ancient religious symbols, rises above the starry universe to link heaven and earth.*

want to follow the exact lunar timings it is better to buy a calendar that is specially prepared and calculated each year.

A YEAR AND A DAY

The addition of an extra or "leap" day every four years during the month of February—which probably stems from Egyptian times—may have given rise to the magical phrase of "a year and a day." It is also possible that the phrase came about during the changeover between ancient and modern methods of calculating specific time

periods. The Romans measured time periods by counting the starting day and ending day; for instance, Monday was three days before Wednesday. Today, we do not use this system, but there are residues in some cultures—the French term, *quinze jours* (fifteen days) refers to a two-week period of fourteen days.

A year and a day has always been considered a very special and magical span of time, used in all sorts of ancient pagan customs such as hand-fasting ceremonies. It includes both the date of the ceremony together with the same date one year later. This length of time was also used in certain legal issues. For example, the Crown had the right to hold the land of criminals for a year and a day. And, as we all know, this is how long the Owl and the Pussycat sailed away for!

MOON AND TREE MAGIC

Moon magic is always associated with tree magic. The tree is regarded as one of the most powerful totems in nature. Its branches stretch upward toward heaven to receive messages, while its roots dig deep into the earth providing protection, food and medicine, and nurturing for both animals and humans, making the bridge between the seen and unseen worlds. Those who practice the Old Ways revere the tree as a truly sacred part of life, using its mystical qualities to empower both magical rites and festive celebrations.

Allegory of the Tree of Life (*Italian mosaic, detail*). *Trees provide a link with the heavens.*

THE CELTIC CALENDAR

The tree was used by the Celts to create a calendar, with the year divided into tree months. The calendar shown here is based on William Morris's *Tree Calendar*, which developed the idea of an earlier Celtic version.

SNOW MOON
Capricorn to Aquarius
Rowan tree: Protection, healing, success

The rowan is often found growing beside ancient sacred sites. Rowan wood was burned to invoke the spirits to take part in battles, and Norse people used it to carve their runic symbols. Many people would plant a rowan tree outside the front door to ward off evil spirits. The rowan is considered the female counterpart to the ash tree because, according to Scandinavian mythology, woman was born from the rowan and man from the ash. It is also said that wherever Druid remains are found, so are those of the rowan tree. Rowans were often planted around stone circles and on power points of ley lines to act as protectors.

DEATH MOON
Aquarius to Pisces (includes Imbolc, February 1)
Ash tree: Protection, prosperity, health

The ash tree is the symbol of rebirth, healing, and the sea. It was thought that the wood had powers to prevent drowning; therefore, oars and slats of boats were made from ash. It can also be used as a protection against snakes because it is said a snake will never crawl over its wood. According to Norse legend, the god Odin hung himself on an ash tree named Yggdrasil, "The World Tree," in order to discover the secrets of the universe, which manifested themselves as runic signs. The magic of ash helps us find our alignment in the world. Wherever the ash, oak, and thorn grow together is the natural habitat of the fairies.

AWAKENING MOON
Pisces to Aries (includes Spring Equinox, March 21)
Alder tree: Healing, calming

The alder tree loves watery glades, though it is traditionally associated with the quality of fire and the passion of Venus. Its bark appears to bleed when it is cut because the sap quickly turns red when exposed to air. Consequently, the alder was said to be highly revered by the Druids who believed it to be a mark of prosperity from the Gods. Witches also recognized the importance of the alder tree and would whittle whistles from its wood to conjure up the north wind. Because of alder's resistance to rot, it is used extensively to build bridges, causeways, and quaysides.

GRASS MOON
Aries to Taurus
Willow tree: Love, protection, healing

The willow is the tree of enchantment, capable of inspiring the highest creative forces. It is also a tree associated with the goddess Persephone, Queen of the Underworld, and therefore has been used in death rites for centuries. The besom, the witch's broom, is traditionally bound with willow because it carries the mystical power of the moon. Willows are usually found weeping into streams and rivers, and their bark contains aspirin, used to reduce pain and fever. Willow will also sprout when a cut branch is simply pushed into the soil.

PLANTING MOON
Taurus to Gemini (includes Beltaine, May 1)
Hawthorn tree: Fertility, happiness, chastity

The appearance of the hawthorn heralds the arrival of summer and is associated with joy, happiness and fertility. People decked their homes with hawthorn blossom to mark a time of pleasure and festivities. The hawthorn is sacred to the fairies and is dedicated to Persephone, Queen of the Underworld, who appears for six months of the year above ground, during the summer months, before she returns once more to Hades, her Lord and King of the Underworld, for the winter months.

ROSE MOON

Gemini to Cancer (includes Summer Solstice, June 21)

Oak tree: Strength, luck, love, potency, health, money

The oak tree was the power totem of the Druids and was central to their teachings. In fact, the word "druid" is said to mean "knowledge of the oak." The Druids believed they could reach the great gateway to the other world through the energetic doorway of the oak. The oak is particularly associated with Thor, the Norse god of thunder, because it is more likely to be struck by lightning than any other tree. Its wood is made into beautiful furniture and robust doors for protection. In Greek mythology, Jason built his ship, the *Argo*, with trees from a sacred oak grove.

LIGHTNING MOON
Cancer to Leo (includes Lammas, August 1)
Hazel tree: Luck, fertility, protection, wishes

The hazel tree has intrinsic magical qualities that are used to divine for water and ley lines. It is regarded as the tree of knowledge, and its nuts are the vessels of wisdom. The expression "in a nutshell" refers to the hazelnut and its innate wisdom. In ancient times the hazel was considered the gateway to the fairy realms and, as such, was called the poet's tree. Druids also used the hazel to invoke invisibility and as a powerful protection amulet. Because of its association with water, fishing rods were often made out of hazel to help the fisherman outwit his prey!

FIRST FRUITS MOON
Leo to Virgo
Apple tree: Love, healing, immortality

The apple symbolizes love, passion, union, and, according to Judaeo-Christian mythology, temptation. In many legends, apples offer the gift of eternal youth. During the festival of Samhain, or Hallowe'en, they are considered to be the food of the dead. However, they also symbolize love and it is said that cutting one in half and sharing it with someone you desire will ensure happiness. The apple tree is dedicated to the goddess Aphrodite because its fruit is one of her sacred symbols. Cut in half, it reveals a five-pointed star, the pentagram, the symbol of humankind. In many pagan festivals, the apple tree was wassailed, or saluted, on the twelfth night to ensure a good crop.

HARVEST MOON
Virgo to Libra (includes Autumn Equinox, September 21)
Vine: Strength, durability, prosperity

The vine was originally brought to Britain by the Belgic Celts; however, because of its need for warmth, it thrives only in the southernmost parts of the country. It is the symbol of bounty, pleasure, and lust. Bacchus, or Dionysus, is the god of wine, revelry, and thoroughly bad behavior, and his crown is traditionally made from the leaves and grapes of the vine, as well as of ivy. In colder regions the hardy blackberry was used as a substitute for vine in many pagan rites and ceremonies. It was customary to make blackberry wine to mark the end of the summer and to provide a warming tipple on a brisk autumnal evening. Sacred Celtic fires were made from rowan, oak, and blackberry.

HUNTER'S MOON
Libra to Scorpio (includes Samhain, October 21)
Ivy: Longevity, lucidity

The ivy plant has a mixed reputation because of its tendency to throttle other trees and plants with its rampaging growth. However, it possesses potent magical powers to attract love and to guard against negativity and disaster. Dionysus crowned himself with ivy to counterattack against the effects of too much wine. An ancient Druidic custom is to present a married couple with a wreath of ivy to bless the union. Traditionally, in the eleventh month of the pagan calendar, the Druids used the evergreen ivy to decorate their sacred sites and altars. Ivy symbolizes everlasting life and is magically paired with holly to represent the male and female principles of life.

TREE MOON

Scorpio to Sagittarius

Yew tree: Raising the dead, everlasting life

Some yew trees are more than three thousand years old and, because of their longevity, are greatly revered by the ancient Wise Ones and are to be found in many ancient sites and churchyards. The yew's ability to propagate its own seed in its trunk gives rise to its reputation of creating everlasting life. It is also associated with dead lovers and is said to spring to life from their graves, as if to mark forever what has been. The "king's wheel" was a circular brooch worn by the monarch as a potent reminder of the cycle of existence and his own mortality. Longbow archers made arrows from yew, and believed that they offered charmed protection in battle.

LONG NIGHT MOON

Sagittarius to Capricorn (including Winter Solstice, December 21 or 22)

Mistletoe: Protection, love, hunting, fertility, health

The Druids looked upon mistletoe, their most sacred herb, as the plant of peace. They believed it fell from heaven onto the oak, and they named its white berries "heal-all," seeing in them a resemblance to semen, which carries the spark of life. The berries were used to cure impotence and infertility. It is unusual for mistletoe to grow on English oaks, so when it did, its rarity ensured it was invested with healing powers. Because mistletoe was associated with the sun, its wood was gathered by one stroke of a golden sickle on the summer solstice. Its berries and leaves were gathered in the same way on the winter solstice. The link between mistletoe and fertility means a kiss under the mistletoe could be very productive!

The Thirteenth Lunar Month:
The Blue Moon

The Blue Moon is the extra or thirteenth lunar month that occurs in an astrological sign every two or three years. It is the nebulous mysterious moon which is thought to incorporate all the hidden magical and mystical powers of the Moon Goddess. The power of the Blue Moon is extremely flexible and it is believed to take on whichever kind of magical attributes that the Goddess feels are called for at that particular time. Likewise, the tree that is associated with the Blue Moon can also change. The trees and plants that are linked with this moon are elder, birch, gorse, blackthorn, heather, holly, poplar, and reed, most of which contain the magical properties of protection, exorcism, healing, and purification.

CHAPTER 4

FESTIVALS AND CELEBRATIONS

A Bacchante (Arthur Hacker). The Earth Mother Goddess was celebrated at the sabbats, which marked the changing seasons.

THE FOUR GREAT PASTORAL SABBATS

The witch's calendar consists of eight important dates called sabbats or festivals. Four of these were originally held to celebrate the farming cycle—the root of society. The origins of the word "sabbat" remain obscure; however, it is most probable that it comes from the Hebrew sabbath meaning "sacred" or "holy." According to another school of thought the word comes from Sabadius, which was the Greek name for Dionysus, the god of wine and revelry.

SAMHAIN: OCTOBER 31

The witch's New Year begins on the great sabbat of Samhain, October 31. This is also known as Allhallows Eve, or more commonly as Hallowe'en. *Samhain* is an old Celtic word meaning "summer's end," and the origins of this festival lie far back in pagan times when the passage of the dead was greatly revered.

During the Samhain festivities, huge bonfires were constructed from all the rubbish in a village and lit for a week to mark the death of summer and the birth of winter. Since Samhain was the night of death it was also a time for people to honor those who had died during the year; among pagans, Samhain was also known as the Festival of the Dead. The people gave thanks to their dearly departed, who they believed still helped them from the spirit world. The bonfires of Samhain had a dual purpose; they not only marked the end of summer but also lit the way for the dead as they journeyed to higher realms. As a mark of respect, people would build altars and pile them high with apples as offerings of thanks. Apples were considered the fruits of

immortality; they were often buried on Samhain so that those souls returning to the mortal world in the spring would have enough food during the cold winter months. Because of this custom, Samhain is also known as the Festival of Apples.

The tradition of hollowing out pumpkins and turnips into dreadful-looking ghouls and ghosts stems from the belief that the night of Samhain is when the veil between the seen and unseen

Eve (Anna Lea Merritt). Apples were gathered at Samhain and offered in thanks to departed souls, whose way was lit by bonfires.

worlds is at its thinnest. The souls of the dead could walk abroad, and so could every other type of goblin and sprite. The lanterns that are created

Hallowe'en (James Elder Christie). One of the few pagan customs that have survived to the present day—making lanterns out of pumpkins at Hallowe'en.

serve to frighten away those unwelcome spirits. The custom of trick-or-treat originates from the belief that such wicked beings could cause havoc at a moment's notice. Children dress up in black costumes and go banging on doors shouting "trick or treat," and sorry are those who are not forthcoming with a treat!

The beautiful ceremony of Samhain, like so many of the pagan celebrations, was appropriated by the Christian Church. They made November 1 All Hallows or All Saints Day. However, this was to have no effect on the long-standing custom of celebrating Allhallows Eve in the traditional fashion, so they eventually removed All Hallows Day from their calendar, only restoring it in the 1920s when they believed the roots of Hallowe'en as a celebration of the dead had been forgotten.

In England today, the bonfires that take place on November 5 have replaced those of Samhain.

On the Road to the Temple of Ceres: A Spring Festival (*Sir Lawrence Alma-Tadema*).
The dark winter days are over and spring is greeted with dancing, flowers, and sensual pleasures.

IMBOLC: FEBRUARY 2

This festival marks the beginning of the ewe's lactation and, therefore, the beginning of a new life cycle. The old name for Imbolc was Oimelc, meaning "ewe's milk." Imbolc was also known as Candlemas, or the Festival of Lights, which celebrates the appearance of snowdrops and their association with purity, innocence, and newness. People would light candles on this day to signify that once again light and warmth had survived through the cold and dark of the winter months. In the old days, Candlemas was the time when winter green foliage, which had been brought into the house as a reminder that nature thrived even though it had disappeared underground, was removed. Imbolc was also a time to celebrate the return of the Goddess from the underworld and so this day was especially sacred for women.

Bridgit, or Bride, of Ireland is the patron goddess of Imbolc, bards, good harvests, healthy babies, and women. Women would take a sheaf of oats, shape and dress it to resemble the female form of Bridgit and hang it beside the fireplace. In the morning they would look to see if her footprints could be found in the ashes of the fire. Such was her hold over Irish women that the Christian Church canonized her as a saint; however, she kept the greatest following among the people of Ireland as their pagan goddess.

Imbolc is traditionally the day when a new witch is initiated into the Old Ways. After a ceremony in which the power and protection of the Goddess is evoked and the witch is symbolically reborn, she is offered honey to "taste the sweetness of the Goddess" and welcome her into the order of initiates.

La Primavera (*Walter Crane*). *Flowers played an important part in every pagan celebration. Snowdrops, the first flowers of the year, were welcomed at "Imbolc," the Festival of Lights.*

BELTAINE: APRIL 30

Beltaine is also known as May Eve, the time when the cattle were driven to their summer pasture and great celebrations took place to mark the beginning of summer. Houses were decked with may or hawthorn blossom, and young girls would wear it in their hair. The word Beltaine comes from Bel, the Celtic sky god, and the Welsh word *tan* meaning "fire." Originally, this day was celebrated by the union between the Stag Lord and the May Queen. These

Women on the Banks of the Nile (*Roman pavement mosaic, detail*). *Beltaine was a time for celebration and love.*

were chosen for their roles from birth. As an initiation into manhood, the Stag Lord would go to face the great stag of the herd and try to overcome him. If the Stag Lord was defeated or killed, there was always a second or standby Stag Lord to take his place. If he returned victorious, the May Queen, who was of approximately the same age, became his bride for the season. Their union brought fertility to the land for the

oncoming summer months, and great honor was heaped upon the couple since they were considered to be the embodiment of the God and Goddess.

Beltaine was also the time for couples to dance around the fire in the act of commitment. The ensuing relationship would last a year and a day, after which time the couple could go their separate ways. Beltaine was a time of great sexual activity, fun, and frolics. Astrologically, this wonderful festival falls into the sensuous sign of Taurus, which is governed by Venus, the planet of love. The moon is at the height of its power in Taurus, which brings even greater powers to the emotions. The Christian Church tried to discourage and discredit these sexual freedoms associated with Beltaine. Yet the maypole still exists, dressed with red ribbons which symbolize the potency of male virility and the fertility of woman, and topped with white flowers and broom, which symbolize the blood and milk of the Goddess. The selection of the May Queen still happens today, but few parents or daughters realize the ancient significance of her role, and many would be horrified should a Stag Lord come in hot pursuit!

Courtiers in Procession on May Day (The Trés Riches Heures of the Duc de Berry *by Pol de Limbourg, detail). May Day celebrations were suppressed by the Christians, who considered them too sensual.*

Ceres (Peruzzi Baldassare). The Saxons offered thanks to Ceres, Goddess of the Harvest, at the Festival of Bread, when summer was at its height. "Lammas" was later to become Harvest Thanksgiving.

LAMMAS: AUGUST 1

This festival is also known as Lughnasagh in commemoration of Lugh, the Celtic sun god who died and was reborn. It marks the time of Lugh's death, when summer in the northern hemisphere is at its height, just before the sun begins to wane and autumn returns once more. The myth of Lugh has its parallel in the legend of the Welsh king Llew who was murdered and then came back to life. This legend also runs remarkably parallel to the story of Christ. Its symbolism is linked to the perpetual

A Dancing Bacchante at Harvest Time (*Sir Lawrence Alma-Tadema*). *With dancing and celebrations, the Goddess of the Harvest and Goddess of the Earth are revered as the corn is gathered in.*

patience, waiting for the rest of the corn to ripen, and trusting that the Great Goddess will provide.

Lammas comes from the Saxon word *blaf-mass*, which means "festival of bread." Great celebrations and thanksgiving offerings were dedicated to Ceres, Goddess of the Harvest, and Demeter, Goddess of the Earth, to ensure a good harvest. In the old days, farmworkers would attend "wakes" to honor the death of the corn god, often carrying hooped wreaths made from corn. Because of the association with the Earth Goddess,

cycle of nature—where there is life, there is death. Both these kings were destined to die for the land, yet rise again, just as winter transforms itself into spring. During this festival, the first corn is harvested or sacrificed to become bread and grain for the winter months. This is also a time of this is a very female festival and therefore a particularly special day for anyone who reveres feminine magic.

The Christian Church transformed these ancient traditions and renamed this festival the Harvest Thanksgiving.

THE FOUR MINOR SABBATS

The four minor sabbats follow the path of the sun, marking the two solstices, when the sun reaches its highest and lowest points, and the two equinoxes, when the sun passes over the equator.

Autumn: Vintage Festival
(*Sir Lawrence Alma-Tadema*). *Fires were lit at the winter solstice to celebrate "the birth of light."*

THE WINTER SOLSTICE

In the northern hemisphere, the winter solstice falls on December 21 or 22, the beginning of Capricorn. This is the shortest day of the year, after which the daylight hours grow longer. Therefore, the winter solstice is known as the "birth of light." The Anglo-Saxon word for this solstice is *yule*, which is derived from the Nordic *iul*, meaning "wheel" as in the sacred circle, or wheel, of nature. This was the day when the chief Druid cut the sacred mistletoe from the oak, allowing it to fall upon a cloak. This tradition is still upheld today when people include mistletoe in their Christmas decorations.

Great fires were lit to celebrate the return of the sun; the "yule" log is the last vestige of this custom. So potent was this Yule festival that the Christian Church adopted December 25 for their own birth celebrations. This was also the date for festivities in honor of the sun god Sol.

The tradition of bringing evergreen holly and ivy into the home during the winter months pays homage to the masculine and feminine elements. The male is the prickly holly with its sexually potent red berries; the female is the entwining, yielding ivy. Together they act as a reminder that nature never dies, but is waiting to be reborn again in the spring.

THE VERNAL EQUINOX

The vernal, or youthful, equinox falls on March 21, the first day of Aries and spring. The sun has reached the equator, so the hours of day and night are equal around the world. This festival is also known as Eostre, in honor of the Anglo-Saxon goddess of spring. Eostre was ceremonially invoked on this day, and it is from her name that the word "Easter" is derived. "East"—the direction of the first light and warmth of the dawning sun—is also derived from the name of the Goddess of Spring. Many witches choose to place their altars facing east in honor of Eostre.

The Christian Church transformed this festival into a time to celebrate the resurrection of Christ. During church services, the priest turns to face the

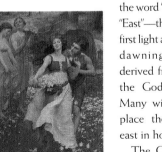

The Progress of Spring *(Charles Daniel Ward, detail). Youth was celebrated at the vernal equinox on the first day of spring.*

Green Summer *(Sir Edward Burne-Jones). Early cultures lived in close harmony with the seasonal cycles of life, growth and death, acknowledging the importance of each turning point in the year.*

east as an expression of belief in Christ as the harbinger of light itself. Church altars are placed in the east to signify the birth and resurrection of Christ, and Christians tend to be buried with their feet pointing eastward in the hope that their souls will be resurrected. The date for Easter Sunday is guided by the moon. It falls on the first Sunday after the Paschal moon—the full moon that occurs either on the equinox or on any of the following 28 days.

THE SUMMER SOLSTICE

In the northern hemisphere, the summer solstice occurs during midsummer on June 21, the time of Cancer and the home. This is the longest day in the year, when the sun has reached its peak, after which daylight hours begin to wane. It is the time of the Celtic goddess Litha, who has the power of abundance, fertility, and order.

And it is on this night that the Druids gathered mistletoe from apple trees. Since the magical quality of the apple tree is love, on this night many people would lie with their lovers in the apple orchards as an expression of devotion to the God and Goddess. The ash tree also played an important part in midsummer celebrations. Eating ash buds was supposed to bring protection from evil intent, and special ale was consumed, which added to the reputation of midsummer madness. This results from the compound effects of a full moon and the heat of the hot sunny days:

What's this, Midsummer moon?
Is all the world gone a-madding?
FROM *AMPHITRYON* BY JOHN DRYDEN

Midsummer was also a time of witchery and pranks, depicted so beautifully in Shakespeare's *A Midsummer Night's Dream.* Great fires of oak wood were lit during the summer solstice in honor of the Goddess of the Hearth and Home, and young lovers would leap the flames. The ashes were scattered among the crops as fertilizer and as an act of homage to the oak king. He was the guardian of the waxing cycle of nature, from midwinter to midsummer. At the time of the summer solstice he sacrificed his reign to the holly king, the lord of the waning cycle of nature, from midsummer to midwinter. Farmers would mark their field boundaries by walking the perimeter with blazing torches in their hands.

Aubergine (*Sanitatis Ortus, detail*). Litha, the Goddess of abundance and fertility, came to power at the Summer Solstice. Young lovers became intoxicated by the full moon, summer sun, and festive ale.

THE AUTUMN EQUINOX

In the northern hemisphere, the autumn equinox is on September 21, in the sign of Libra and balance. It is the time to gather in the last harvest and to honor the dying hours of daylight. According to ancient Greek legend, the goddess Persephone returns to the dark realms of the underworld and to her lord and master, Hades. Demeter, Goddess of the Earth, enters into deep mourning at the loss of her daughter, and everything above ground begins to die. As the leaves begin to turn, it is the perfect time to gather berries and fruit, especially sloes for sloe gin.

Corn dolls were made around this time to pay homage to the spirit of the corn king. The word "dolly" is derived from the word "idol" meaning deity of worship. Corn dolls were either made in the image of the Earth Mother or fashioned into pagan symbols of sexual prowess, such as horns or cornucopias. Sometimes the dolls were made using only seven stalks of corn because of the magical significance of this number.

In the past, the harvest supper was held when the final sheaves of corn had been safely stored. The harvesters would return home singing the harvest home song, and there would be a huge feast for all who had helped to bring in the harvest. The last sheaf of corn was made into

Midsummer Eve (*Edward Robert Hughes*). *Witchcraft took place during midsummer and the Oak King was honored as he gave way to the Holly King and the coming winter.*

Harvest Moon *(Samuel Palmer, detail).*
Workers gather in the last of the corn. The departed
spirit of the Corn King was honored with
corn "dollies," still made today.

the likeness of the Goddess and presented to the winner of the harvest running race. It hung by the victor's fireplace until spring. The harvest moon is the full moon nearest the equinox. It rises for several days around the same time, almost sunset, and therefore provides longer moonlit evenings than at any other time of the year.

Ebats

Ebats take place every month on the full moon. The word comes from the French *s'ebattre,* meaning to frolic and have a good time. Those who revere the Old Ways meet together either as an organized witches' coven of 13 members, one for each of the 13 full moons, or as a gathering of friends wishing to perform some sort of celebration ritual.

Originally, these private meetings took place under the cover of darkness, in woods and forests whenever possible. Being close to the elements is important to the practice of the Old Crafts, which is why many witches perform ceremonies "sky-clad," or naked, out in the open. It is a gesture of innocence as well as a return to nature.

The ebats are where the witches perform their obligatory magical rites and exchange news and views. These ritual meetings are also the occasion for important celebrations such as hand-fastings (weddings) and the presentation of newborn babes to the God and Goddess. There is usually dancing, feasting, and singing. The Christian Church frowned on these secret meetings. And because ebats were often held in the dark hours in the depth of woods and forests where few dare to tread, rumors began to spread of terrible happenings led by the devil himself.

Today, with the growing interest in the Old Ways, many people from all walks of life gather together on the night of the full moon to perform magical rituals and to drum their thanks to the Goddess. It is a delightful thing to do, and easy to organize. These meetings help to slow the hectic pace of modern life, if only for a few hours, by helping us to reconnect with ourselves. They also keep us in touch with the Old Crafts and remind us to respect nature and each other.

Part Two

SYMBOLISM AND THE OLD CRAFTS

CHAPTER 5

WITCHCRAFT AND MAGIC

Indian Ritual Dance from the Village of Secoton (*John White, book illustration*). *Ritual dancing was performed to connect with the spirits of ancestors, sacred animals, and the natural elements.*

The word "magic" comes from the ancient Middle Eastern word *magi* or *magus*, the literal translation of which is "wise man" or "priest." The spelling of "magik" with a k is traditional among practitioners of the Old Crafts. Its origins are Greek, and the word "magik" was incorporated into Middle English as early as the 1300s. This traditional spelling has been retained by those in the Crafts to differentiate between the Arts and the sensational, rabbit-out-of-a-hat stage illusionist's acts.

The craft of magic-making is an ancient one, woven into every facet of life to ensure survival. In our modern society, however, we have no need to fight for our lives or to ask the elements to help us find food and water. But because of this progress in material terms, our ancient connection with the land and the natural elements has diminished. The loss of contact with the natural elements means we have also lost contact with an immensely important part of ourselves, and consequently we behave as if we are separate from the environment rather than part of it. In the process we have also become separate from that other world beyond the veil, the world of spirit.

Those who still live in tribal communities, such as the Aborigines of Australia and the Native Americans, know better. They understand and can work with the natural forces within the environment and also with the spirits of their ancestors and their totem animals. The Aboriginal dream-time is as real and important as their daily routine; one cannot be separated from the other. And it is from this other dream-time reality that the magic springs forth.

Some form of belief in witchcraft exists in all lands, from earliest times to the present day. The art of spell-making, or witchcraft, is a very powerful and beautiful way to reconnect with this other life that runs parallel with our own outer realities. However, as with all things, it must be approached with reverence and respect, otherwise it can lead to all manner of problems.

There is another dimension which coexists with the material world. We can enter it through witchcraft, but this can only be done with love, humility, and a desire for truth. Our inner thinking will always shape our outer reality.

Gypsies (*Charles Robertson*). *As we travel along the road of life, we often need to stop a while to reassess who we are, and what we want to achieve.*

MAGIC AND THE MIND

Magic is created through intent of thought. Therefore, as all witches will tell you, understanding how you tick is one of the most important steps in learning how to work with magic. But before we go into how to channel thoughts and magic so that we can manifest what we wish in our lives, it is important to understand how magic works.

The mind or intellect is the most powerful facility we possess. How we think is who we are.

Therefore everything in our outer reality is a direct reflection on our inner thought processes; we are constantly creating our own realities, both consciously and subconsciously. This concept is very difficult to accept because it seems that we are often the unwitting and unwilling victims to all sorts of difficult, painful, and unpleasant situations. But these negative circumstances are merely acting as reminders that we are not approaching life from a state of love and light. When we examine our thought processes and behavior patterns with honesty and humility, we can begin to see a more positive way forward. I personally believe that people are constantly being presented with the opportunities to change their ways. But not everyone has the courage or incentive to grasp those opportunities.

In order to change the negative aspects of our lives, we must first face our deep-rooted feelings of self-hatred. Self-hatred is the root of our destruction; feelings of unworthiness can lead us into the darkest part of ourselves. When we are able to replace self-hatred with love and acceptance, the healing process begins and the world around us takes on a more positive hue.

This self-examination is a life-long task. It's like peeling an onion; each time we have reached a plateau of understanding, another layer of the onion is revealed. However, it is by delving further and further into the darkness that the light can shine brighter and brighter. This is the true role of darkness. Light cannot manifest without it, nor the human soul grow without it. When our soul begins to awaken to the light, we know instinctively that something "good" has happened, that something loving is taking place, and life will never be quite the same again.

If you conduct your ritual work with love and respect, extraordinary and astounding inner visions and "journeys" can often

Good and Evil: The Devil
Tempting a Young Woman
(Andre Jacques Victor Orsel, detail).
*Natural law dictates that the evil
forces of black magic will always
return to their original source.*

occur, taking you to places with profoundly life-altering results. So make sure you go carefully at first and be prepared to meet an inner world that is truly magnificent.

BLACK MAGIC

Some people choose to use their minds and their magic to manipulate the darkness for their own ends. Please understand, there are no "powers of darkness," only manifestations created within the mind; however, these can appear to be very real indeed. Using magic for dark purposes is known as black magic, and it has no genuine connection with the Old Crafts, or the Craft of the Wise. Black magicians can indeed perform extraordinary feats, but at a terrible price. It is the law of the universe that what you put out returns with ten times as much force; therefore, people who work with the black arts are deeply unhappy, self-destructive souls who live restless and tormented lives. To cast a hex or a curse is an extremely dangerous thing to do on a karmic level. The perpetrator will carry the repercussions of this action through every incarnation until he or she rights that wrong.

Since we create our own reality, be constantly vigilant of how you think. Look at how your outer reality is manifesting through circumstances and the people you have drawn into your life. Stay clear of people who wish to control or manipulate you, or use you against your will. Learn from your experiences and mistakes, and follow your inner instincts. This will lead you into the light, even though the path may sometimes bend and weave on the way. Should you feel that you may have been drawn to people who work with the dark forces, immediately ask for help and protection from your spirit guides. Say prayers and mantras to break the connection, and if necessary seek help from professional counselors and healers. But take heart, true wisdom will come from experience.

HEALING AND THE CRAFT OF THE WISE

The Craft of the Wise is concerned entirely with healing, be it animal, vegetable, or mineral. Practitioners who work in the Old Ways know that every single thing on the planet has its own life force. They can tap into, harness, and use their life force for the benefit of others, either through physical contact or through absent healing. Thought becomes the channel for this life force, directing its flow to wherever it is needed. In ancient times, I believe the Wise Ones used ley lines in the land to send all manner of telepathic information to different parts of the

Morgan le Fay: Queen of Avalon (*Anthony Frederick Augustus Sandys*). *Protect yourself from those you suspect of practicing black magic. Your inner wisdom will guide you.*

Orante (*Sir Lawrence Alma-Tadema*). *Your mind can be used as a powerful channel for absent healing as you learn to connect with the life force and direct it where it is needed.*

country and even different parts of the world. The Aborigines use their "song-lines" in the same way. Today, we in the modern world have lost the knowledge to do this; even so, many great healers are still able to achieve phenomenal results just by transmitting healing thoughts telepathically.

DEVIC REALMS AND THE FOUR DIRECTIONS

Those who practise the Craft of the Wise understand instinctively that the natural world is constantly providing us with a rich array of information and helping in every facet of life. They see the world as pulsating with life and filled with devic entities who act as "custodians" within the animal, vegetable, and mineral kingdoms. The four elements—earth, air, fire, and water—and the four directions—north, south, east, and west—are taken into consideration in the practice of the Craft. They represent certain attributes within ourselves and therefore play a very important role when you are conducting any form of magical ritual.

When you open up to the possibility that these entities actually exist, the entire world becomes a very magical place indeed. The wind is no longer just a gust; it carries a personality or spirit. Likewise, a river or stream carries its own individual spirit entities, as does every tree, flower, and herb. When you link with the devic realms, all sorts of extraordinary things occur. For example, those who talk to their garden plants and pour love into them find themselves blessed with an abundance of color, fragrance and beauty. A fire can be lit in difficult conditions by speaking to the salamander spirits. The water devas can prevent someone from drowning against all odds.

The Elements: Water *(Jan Breughel).*
The undines, guardians of the water element, the west, autumn, and the color blue, represent the setting sun, the place of dreams, inner visions, and journeys.

All those traditions that honor the earth also pay homage in one way or another to the four directions, the four elements of earth, air, fire, and water, and to the four devic realms. Practitioners of the Old Crafts usually incorporate a variation of the following in their rites:

The Elements: Air *(Jan Breughel).* The air element is guarded by the sylphs, who also preside over the east, spring, and the color yellow. They represent intellect, illumination, clear thinking, and creation.

The Elements: Earth *(Jan Breughel). Gnomes guard the earth element, the north, winter, and the color green. They also symbolize the abundance, fertility, and prosperity of the material world.*

The sylphs—guardians of the east, air, spring, and yellow—represent intellect, illumination, clear thinking, and creation. East is the gateway to new beginnings.

The salamanders—guardians of the south, fire, summer, and red—represent the inner child, inspiration, fire, passion, and change. South is the gateway to creativity.

The undines—guardians of the west, water, autumn, and blue—represent the direction of the setting sun, the place of dreams, inner visions, and journeys. West is the gateway to the emotions.

The gnomes—guardians of the north, earth, winter, and green—represent the physical world, abundance, fertility, and prosperity. North is the gateway to wisdom, knowing, and the mind.

THE SACRED WHEEL OF LIFE

Most magical traditions lay out symbols of the four directions in a specific order that creates a sacred circle. This circle acts as a reminder that human existence is a continuous wheel of experience, which we all must tread for many lifetimes until we have worked out the karma of our existence. It symbolizes life, death, and rebirth. When laying out a circle follow this ritual pattern:

☾ First, pay homage to the sylphs of the east since this is where illumination takes place.

☾ Second, pay homage to the salamanders of the south since this is the place of innocence.

☾ Third, pay homage to the undines of the west since this is the place of inner visions.

☾ Lastly, pay homage to the gnomes of the north since this is the place of physical manifestation.

The Elements: Fire *(Jan Breughel). The warmth of the south, fire, summer, and the color red are the province of the salamanders, who stand for the child within, inspiration, and change.*

Witches normally work with altars, often placing them to face north—the gateway to earth and manifestation. When working with a large circle, it is usually entered from the direction of the east. However, as with all things, I suggest you trust your own intuition on this. Place your

Four Ages of Life (Pietro da Cortona). Rituals can enhance your life, whatever your age.

altar wherever it feels comfortable. Even if you are not drawn to working with the devic energies or altars and symbols, I believe it is very important to pay homage to the Earth Mother when performing any type of ritual. She supports and nurtures us without wrangle, no matter what we do to her. Unless we give something back, the ritual becomes a one-way street, and it is unlikely that the magic will work. The whole of the universe exists in circular motion so unless there is a flow of giving and receiving, the circle cannot exist. Certainly you may draw things to you when you conduct a ritual based solely on desire for personal gain, but when this desire comes from the selfishness of the ego your ritual is unlikely to manifest harmonious experiences.

Wise practitioners know how to become one with the universal consciousness lovingly and unreservedly and ask only for manifestations that are for the good of themselves and those connected to them. When this happens, the universe creates what is needed at the precise moment it is required. And that is the real magic talking.

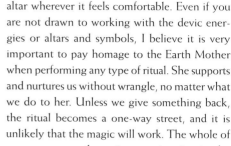

The Wheel of Fortune (French book illustration). The Wheel of Life stands for the many lifetimes we may need to go through in order to learn the lessons given to us.

CHAPTER 6

THE SYMBOLISM OF NUMBERS

Just as candles and incense play important roles in ritual work, numbers and their symbols also have deep significance. In the words of Helen Blavatsky, the founder of the Theosophical Society, "Numbers underlie form, and numbers guide sound. It lies at the root of the manifested universe."

Before we discuss the symbols of numbers, we need to understand the effect that symbols have on us, and why they were created.

Our relationship with the Infinite, God, the Cosmos, the Great Creator—there are many names for the Divine—can only be

Astrologers Casting Horoscopes during Celebrations for the Birth of Timur (*Akbar Nama* scene). *Astrology and alchemy cannot provide all the answers. We need to seek the truth within ourselves.*

runes. Organized religion came into being to help us understand and find our way back to the Infinite. But ultimately, it is only through our own inner self or higher consciousness that we can make contact with the Infinite, and it is a constant struggle to make that link because of the power of our own egos. To be one with the Infinite, the ego must be set aside.

Because symbols are the language of the Divine, they act for the higher consciousness, operating beyond the ego and the intellect. Numbers and their symbols hold ancient meanings that have

expressed symbolically. Since the dawn of time, people have tried to understand and explain this relationship through mythology, ancient texts, and scriptures such as the Cabbala and the Vedas, the sciences of astrology and alchemy, and symbols such as the tarot, numerology, and the

been used for centuries by all sorts of religions as well as by those who practice the Old Crafts. They are a vital element in ritualistic work. However, it is very important to understand their meanings, otherwise using them is like trying to speak a language without understanding its grammar.

Numbers are at the heart of universal order and
they help us make a connection with the truth
beyond our own egos. We need symbols to
describe the infinite and an understanding of
these is vital to ritual work. First, therefore, we
need to learn their language.

NUMBERS AND THEIR SYMBOLS

✱ 1 ✱

One symbolizes the divine spark and is associated with the sun. This number is represented by a circle with a dot in the center, which stands for the center of infinity, the seed, or germ.

This is the symbol for the male principle, the father, the unity of God, the Supreme Intelligence, the self, the original action of God, the original number. There is one sun, one heart, one philosopher's stone, one sovereign prince of the underworld—Lucifer. One is the only number that can be multiplied by itself without changing its value.

Magically, the number one and its symbol represent ambition and courage.

✱ 2 ✱

Two symbolizes differentiation and is associated with the moon. This number is represented by an angle, illustrating the descent—or fall —into matter.

This is the symbol for the female principle; the Goddess, the unconscious. It represents the duality of humanity and the Divine, the spirit and the flesh. It is the sign of marriage, motherhood, and childbirth. It also symbolizes mystery, occult matters, and money.

Magically, the number two and its symbol represent the emotions, harmony, cooperation, and wealth. By discovering the law of two that operates all around us, we can unify our lives.

Primavera *(Sandro Botticelli, detail). The number two, associated with the moon,
is symbolic of the female principle, mystery, money, and the occult.*

∗ 3 ∗

Three symbolizes manifestation and is associated with the planet Jupiter. This number is represented by a triangle. When it points upward it symbolizes fire, light, and heavenly powers. When it points downward it symbolizes water, darkness, and humanity's baser instincts.

SYMBOL UP

SYMBOL DOWN

This is the symbol for the holy trinity of wisdom, love, and truth. In Christianity, three represents the Father, Son, and Holy Ghost. Three is a most sacred number, representing the physical manifestation in life, the triangle of our intellect, heart, and body. "Knock on the door of heaven three times, and it shall be open unto you."

Magically, the number three and its symbol represent creativity, joy, and expansion.

Jesus Flees Damascus with Two Angels
(Turkish miniature). The sacred number three, when pointing upwards, is the symbol for fire, light, and heavenly power.

∗ 4 ∗

Four symbolizes the earth and is associated with the planet Uranus. This number is represented by a square because it unites the four ends of the cross.

However, the following symbols are also used in connection with the number four:

The circle with the quaternary. The sacred square also represents the four elements, the four corners of the heavens, and the four evangelists. Within the square lies the circle of infinity. Thus the cosmos is contained within the earth, just as the earth is part of the entire cosmos.

The cosmic cross, both shows the descent of spirit into matter, and its ascent. The vertical line represents the active, dynamic principle; the horizontal line the passive, static, earthly principle. We all undergo "sacrifice" when our spirit enters into the material plane; therefore, the cosmic cross represents the struggle that we invariably incur during our earthly life as we seek the true way toward spiritual enlightenment.

The Christian cross represents the agony and martyrdom of Christ. However, it also represents the innate desire of the soul to ascend toward enlightenment as well as symbolizing the afterlife.

The ankh is the Egyptian hiero-
glyphic for the key of life and
immortality. The circle represents the higher planes;
however, it is elongated because
once the soul enters into the material world it is
no longer wholly divine.

The serpent and the cross is a very
ancient occult symbol described
in the Old Testament. It demon-
strates humanity's need to rise
above the nature of desire in
order to become one with God. A version of this
symbol is used as the emblem of the medical
fraternity. The sacred square gives form to life—
the four seasons, the four elements, the four
cardinal directions, the four elemental spirits.
There are the four horses of the Apocalypse, the
four evangelists—Matthew, Mark, Luke, and
John; the four holy creatures who guard the
throne of God (human/air, eagle/water, lion/fire,
bull/earth); and also the four hallows of grail,
stone, sword, and wand.

Magically, the number four and its symbol
represent will, discipline, and construction.

* 5 *

Five symbolizes humanity and is associated with
the planet Mercury. This number is represented
by the five-pointed star, which is known as the
star of the magi.

This is an extremely potent symbol and is used,
pointing upward, in magical rites as a protection
against evil influences. It represents the five
emanations of the physical person—the mind,
the word, intelligence, wisdom, and strength; and
the five senses—taste, smell, hearing, sight, and
touch. There are five points in the pentagram,
five marks of the stigmata, and five digits of the
hands and feet which, in pairs, reflect the ten
commandments.

Magically, the number five and its symbol
represent freedom, mental dexterity, and communication. Five is also the symbol of fruitfulness
and new learning.

Radiant Moon (*Edward Robert Hughes, detail*).
*The mythical four horses of the Apocalypse are
representative of the sacred four-sided square that
gives form to life.*

⚹ 6 ⚹

Six symbolizes beauty and is associated with the planet Venus. This number is represented by Solomon's seal, the six-pointed star.

This is the symbol for the human soul as a union of the conscious and unconscious mind. Its two triangles are symbols of perfect balance between the spiritual and physical worlds. It is also known as the Star (or shield) of David. It is the Hindu symbol for the god Vishnu. Pythagoras used it as a symbol of creation. The ancient Egyptians used it to represent generation.

Six is the number of creation and perfection, and also the number of responsibility: "Six days shalt thou labor." There are six points of Christian ritual—the altar lights, the vestments, the chalice, incense, unleavened bread, and the eastward direction of worship. It is the sign of feminine love, pregnancy, and healing.

Magically, the number six and its symbol represent love, wisdom, and responsibility.

The King's Seal *(Egyptian wall painting). The ancient Egyptian ankh symbol, found on the walls of pharaohs' tombs, is connected with the number four and stands for the key of life and immortality.*

✳ 7 ✳

Seven symbolizes perfect order and is associated with the planet Neptune. This number is represented by a six-pointed star with a dot in its center, which stands for the six days of creation, with God or the Creator at its core.

In Jewish traditions the number seven is represented by Ternary—the seven-branched candlestick.

Seven is the highest mystical and sacred number. It represents life because it contains the four elements of the body—spirit, flesh, bone, and humor—together with the three elements of the soul—passion, desire, and reason. The Divine is symbolized by three higher centers of the body—crown, third eye, and throat—and the earth by the four lower centers—the heart, solar plexus, reproductive organs, and coccyx.

There are seven days in creation, seven days in a week, seven graces, seven years of the lunar completion cycle, seven wonders of the world, the seven chakras of the body, the seven notes of the musical scale, and the seven oceans of the world. It is the ancient number of cosmic order.

Magically the number seven and its symbol represent higher learning, spirituality, and contemplation.

· 8 ·

Eight symbolizes strength and is associated with the planet Saturn. This number is represented by the figure of the eight. This is the symbol of the spiraling motion of the creative forces or what is known in the East as the *kundalini* or life-force energy. It also represents karmic justice, "as above, so below."

When placed on its side, this is the mark of infinity, representing regeneration and resurrection. It provides the circuit through which the spirit can dissolve into matter and vice versa.

The number eight is also represented by the hourglass and the scales of justice, which symbolize the balance of spirit and matter, and discipline.

It is said that the number eight is the oldest primary number; this belief comes from an Arab fable which tells of a man meditating on the secret of life. A snake came to him and wrote the shape of the eight in the sand, completing it by swallowing its own tail, as a symbol of eternity.

Magically, the number and its symbol represent divine law, authority, and materialism. It can also stand for the potential of blending the male and female principles into harmonious integration through self-awareness, strength, and courage.

· 9 ·

Nine signifies completeness and is associated with the planet Mars. This number symbolizes the circle of spirit (the circle) made manifest of the earth plane (the straight line).

The number nine—a circle with a tail—echoes the shape of a sperm and therefore symbolizes the male sexual force that transforms spirit into matter.

The number nine is symbolized by the mystic rose, with nine petals on the outer edge, six in the second row and three in its center.

There are nine orders of angels in three triads: seraphim, cherubim, thrones; dominions, virtues, powers; principalities, archangels, angels. There are nine rivers of hell, and the descent to earth of the fallen angel took nine days. Nine is the trinity of trinities: one trinity represents perfect unity; twice three represents perfect duality; three times three represents the perfect plural. Jews use the ninth day of every month to fast and repent. Christ died on the cross at the ninth hour.

Nine is the end of the numerical series before returning to unity; therefore, it is the end of the cycle. Nine is indestructible when multiplied or added to its own multiple; therefore, it is the alpha and the omega, the beginning and the end.

Magically, nine and its symbol represent unconditional service, action, and physical prowess. Major life changes are often dictated in nine-year cycles, the ninth year being a period of letting go of the old in order to allow the new to formulate.

✳ 0 ✳

The cipher is associated with the planet Pluto.

This is the sacred circle and symbol of perfection. It is the secret mystery and the great void. It contains all things and therefore is the number or shape of protection as well as the infinite.

✳ 10 ✳

Ten symbolizes perfection through completeness.

The number ten symbolizes the return to unity, the accomplishment of purpose. The cipher, or zero, represents humanity's vast unmanifested potential, which is accessible by using the rod of power—the divine creative spirit.

The circle divided by a straight line symbolizes the unmanifested being cut in half to manifest as a universe of polarity or pairs of opposites such as heaven and earth, night and day, man and woman, love and hate.

Magically, the number ten and its symbol represent transformation.

Inscribed Bronze Divining Disk of Pergamon. *Used in ancient divining rituals, the circle of this sacred artefact represents infinity and the great void of humankind's unrealized potential.*

· 11 ·

Eleven symbolizes new beginnings. This number is represented by two rods that signify a new and more advanced cycle of manifestation, which has gained much wisdom through experience of the previous cycle.

In numerologists' terms, eleven is the master number on the physical plane; 22 is mastery on the mental plane through the development of reason and diplomacy; 33 is mastery on the spiritual plane from the desire gained for a higher level of service.

Magically, the number eleven and its symbol represent a higher level of understanding.

The Aged Mullah *(Mughal miniature). Mental and spiritual wisdom are the rewards of old age and lessons learned in present and past lives. These higher qualities are represented by the number eleven.*

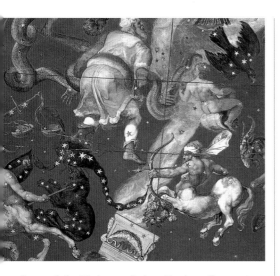

Signs of the Zodiac including Battling Centaurs
(*Giovanni de Vecchi, detail from the vault of the Hall of the World Maps*). *Cosmic order is expressed by the twelve signs of the zodiac.*

✳ **12** ✳

Twelve symbolizes cosmic order. This number is represented by the wheel, which is symbolic of cosmic order and spiritual perfection.

Twelve is the number of spokes that make up the wheel of life—the zodiac. The zodiac is probably the most ancient and sacred concept of divine manifestation within creation. The circle is made from the four-fold expression of earth, air, fire, and water; the wheel embodies continuation; the spokes express spirit in manifested form. Its symbolism is used in many ways: there were twelve sons of Jacob, twelve tribes of Israel, twelve apostles, twelve knights of the round table, twelve precious stones of the breastplate, twelve labors of Hercules, and twelve sacred cushions of the Japanese deity.

Magically, the number twelve and its symbol represent perfection.

Labors of the Months (*Medieval manuscript illustration*).
The twelve months of the year turn full circle, symbolizing continuity and perfection.

CHAPTER 7

SYMBOLIC ORACLES

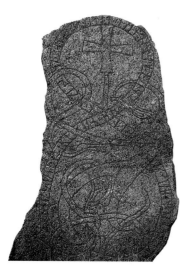

Eleventh-Century Rune Stone (*Gustavium Garden, Uppsala*). *The powerful messages given by rune stones can help guide us on our journey through life.*

THE RUNES

One of the oldest known systems of symbols is that of the runes. It is said that the Norse god Odin, having wounded himself with his sword, hung from Yggdrasil, the Tree of the World, for nine days and nights to receive the wisdom of the world, which appeared in the form of individual runic symbols. The word rune means "mystery" or "secret," and aptly so, because each has a powerful meaning that puts us in touch with the secret or hidden parts of ourselves. The runes are a powerful oracle.

Runes shalt thou find
and fateful signs
That the king of singers colored
and the mighty gods have made;
Fall strong the signs
that the ruler of the gods doth write.

HAVAMAL, AN ANCIENT RUNIC SAGE

In practical terms, the runes have been used in one form or another since the second century. The Goths created the symbols from the Greek and Latin written script, giving each a name which resonated to the sign and they were used as a form of alphabet.

By the fourth century, the use of runes had spread to Germany and other German-speaking countries in Europe. In Scandinavia, the runes were still being used up until the eighteenth century. Historically, the use of runic magic was a closely guarded secret because it was said that the dead could be brought back to life, such was their power. However, today there has been an explosion of interest in these wonderful ancient symbols and many people use them for their own personal form of divination and guidance.

By uncovering the hidden truths in our
subconscious selves we can start the healing
and growing process. Runes can help
unlock our awareness—make a simple set
for yourself by drawing the signs on small
pieces of wood or stones.

life ✳ MAGiC

RUNIC SIGNS

THE SELF	PARTNERSHIP	SIGNALS	SEPARATION
STRENGTH	INTUITION	CONSTRAINT	FERTILITY
DEFENSE	PROTECTION	POSSESSION	JOY
HARVEST	OPENING	WARRIOR	GROWTH
MOVEMENT	FLOW	DISRUPTION	COMMUNICATION
GATEWAY	BREAKTHROUGH	STANDSTILL	WHOLENESS
			THE UNKNOWABLE

*Each symbol has a special and powerful message for those
who wish to hear. It is important to make a full study of the
runic signs for their use in ritual work.*

There are quite a few forms of runic symbolism, mainly derived from Germanic, Scandinavian, and Anglo-Saxon lineage. For the purpose of simplicity, I am using the Viking runes developed by Ralph Blum, a runic master of considerable note and the author of *The Book of Runes* which I highly recommend (see Further Reading).

For divination, tune into the aspect of your life that requires guidance and then choose a rune.

Philosophers of the Ancient World—Solon (Sixteenth-century fresco, detail). The ancient philosophers had special wisdom and insights which are largely disregarded in modern times.

The symbol of the rune you have selected will indicate what you are experiencing in your life at this moment. For example, if you draw the "growth" rune, then any venture you undertake at this time should be successful. However, if you draw the "standstill" or "disruption" rune, then your venture is postponed until a more auspicious time. The following is a list of runic signs that are very useful when used as personal talismans:

PROSPERITY

HEALING

LOVE

JOY

ALPHABETS

The runic alphabet is often used to carve powerful empowerment inscriptions onto magical objects such as wands and staffs. There are a number of different runic alphabets which are used by practitioners of the Old Crafts, all of which are spelt phonetically.

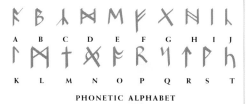

PHONETIC ALPHABET

There are many magical alphabets in existence, but I want to mention two in particular. The first is the Theban alphabet, which originated with the ceremonial magicians, probably in the early Middle Ages when many practitioners of magic had to use secret codes to protect themselves. It is now widely used by witches all over the world:

THEBAN ALPHABET

The second magical alphabet is the Ogham alphabet, which dates back to the time of the Druids. It is named after Ogamus, the Gaulish god of speech. However, it is also believed by many that this alphabet forms the written language of Atlantis:

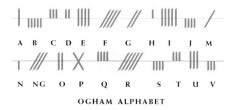

OGHAM ALPHABET

GENERAL SYMBOLS

Symbolism is such a rich area that it would take a lifetime to explore in any depth, but I include here a few of my personal favorites for you to incorporate into your own life if you so wish.

IMPREGNABLE DEFENSE
Deflect instrusion

TWIN HEARTS
Binding love

THE TREE OF LIFE
Ancient wisdom

BIND KNOT
Magical enclosure

HEAVEN PILLAR
Eternal stability

THE GODDESS FREA'S SIGN
Healthy sexuality

OLD SCRATCH GATE
Blocking negative energies

POWER
The rising sun

THE RUNNING EIGHT
Boundary protection of thresholds

THE EYE
Protection against evil

Figure of Om.
There are many different names and symbols for God. Every culture has its own.

OM

Om is the Hindu symbol for God and many people wear this symbol without realizing the significance of it.

Each part of the symbol Om represents a part of us:
1. The outer world; 2. The inner world;
3. The innermost world, the part of ourselves that is totally private; 4. The realization that we are part of the divine consciousness, which has no boundaries and cannot be contained on any level; 5. The center of the ultimate beingness, the "isness" of the divine.

THE TAROT

The origins of the tarot have been lost in the distant past. There are two sections to the tarot: the major arcarna and the minor arcarna.

The major arcarna contains 22 cards that symbolize the 22 pathways to enlightenment, and is based on the Cabbala, the ancient Hebrew teachings. The minor arcarna contains 56 cards divided into four suits symbolizing the four natural elements of earth/materialism, air/intellect, fire/inspiration, and water/emotions. Together, the two sections contain 78 cards. The oldest, most complete pack is the Italian Visconti deck, which dates back to around 1450. The original cards were unnamed and unnumbered and did not include the Tower and the Devil. They were laid out in a different sequence to that used today.

The tarot offers an extremely rich and rewarding way of gaining powerful insights into your life. Like the runes, the tarot can be used as an oracle and as a guide to understanding the inner self. Only through in-depth study can you receive the full benefit of the tarot, and this is something I would highly recommend to anyone interested in the Old Crafts.

THE MAGICIAN   JUNON   THE EMPRESS   THE EMPEROR   JUPITER

THE LOVERS   THE CHARIOT   JUSTICE   THE HERMIT   WHEEL of FORTUNE   STRENGTH

THE HANGED MAN   DEATH   TEMPERANCE   THE DEVIL   THE TOWER   THE STAR

THE MOON   TYE SUN   JUDGEMENT   THE WORLD   FOOL

Not just a game of chance. Like the runes, tarot cards—once fully studied and understood— can reveal important messages and insights to help us go forward in our lives.

CHAPTER 8

ASTROLOGY

The astrologer's ephemeris, which gives all the exact timings of the daily placements of the planets, is an important tool for any witch. The word "planet" comes from the Greek *planetes*, meaning "wanderer," and the movement of these heavenly wanderers can determine the most auspicious time to conduct a ritual. However, if you are a beginner in the Crafts, don't worry too much about this now. In time, if this is to be your path, you will automatically be drawn into learning about astrology. What I offer here is a brief introduction to the subject.

The zodiac wheel, as the occult symbol of the number 12, has already been discussed. Its name has Greek origins and literally means "sculptured figure of an animal." The zodiac itself, is an imaginary belt of stars within our Milky Way galaxy. This band is divided into 12 sections—the 12 signs of the zodiac—each named after the dominant constellation in that section. Within the zodiac the planets are constantly changing their position in relation to the Earth and each other. The movement of these planets form the basis of the science of astrology.

Astrology dates back thousands of years and was certainly used by the ancient Babylonians, Chaldeans, Egyptians, and Sumerians. Because of the powerful, uncontrollable, and often uncomfortable effects that the sun, moon, and stars had upon people's daily lives, the heavens were viewed as the home for all their various gods and goddesses. The major deities became associated with particular planets to reflect their personalities. Thus the zodiac became the symbolic representative of the infinite relationship between humanity and the Divine. In the words of Michael Scott (d. 1235), from his *Liber Introductius*, "Every astrologer is worthy of praise and honor, because he has found favor with God, his Maker, since by such a doctrine as his astronomy he probably knows many secrets of God, and things which few know." By discovering our astrological make-up, we can learn to rise above it.

Indian Star Map: Jewel of Essence of all Sciences
(*Sanskrit manuscript*). *By studying the movements of the planets we can calculate the best time for a particular magic ritual.*

Celestial Map of the Planets, According to Ptolemy (*Georg Christoph Eimmart II*). *Space technology has increased vastly in 2,000 years, but it offers no spiritual insight—such insight can be gained, however, through a study of the stars.*

THE SCIENCE OF ASTROLOGY

The planets represent different facets of our human psyche and, depending on their placement at the moment of birth, they give form to our personalities. Astrology is an exacting mathematical science, and it takes years of study and practice to grasp the full implications it has upon us as individuals. Its influences permeate every facet of our lives and constantly drive us forward, whether we like it or not.

Nostrodamus (1503-66), the french physician and astrologer, is considered by many to be the most famous of all astrologers. His predictions were certainly based on his study of the planets. Hippocrates (c. 460-357 BC), the father of modern medicine, said of astrology, "A physician without a knowledge of astrology has no right to call himself a physician." Rumi, a thirteenth-century Sufi master, said, "Beneath this wheel of stars, your sleep has been heavy. Observe that heaviness. Beware! For life is fragile and quick."

The 12 sun signs perfectly reflect the duality and polarization of human existence:

1ST SIGN	ARIES	*The warrior*
7TH SIGN	LIBRA	*The peacemaker*
2ND SIGN	TAURUS	*Sensuality, beauty*
8TH SIGN	SCORPIO	*Sexuality, desire*
3RD SIGN	GEMINI	*Letters, writing, communication, speech*
9TH SIGN	SAGITTARIUS	*Knowledge, books, travel*
4TH SIGN	CANCER	*Home*
10TH SIGN	CAPRICORN	*Career*
5TH SIGN	LEO	*The ego, self*
11TH SIGN	AQUARIUS	*The group*
6TH SIGN	VIRGO	*Practical work, physical health*
12TH SIGN	PISCES	*Spiritual practice*

The nine planets and the sun represent aspects of our psyche, and their glyphs, all of which are based on the circle, crescent, and cross are symbolic of a higher spiritual meaning.

If you want to understand yourself, get your chart done by a professional astrologer. Knowing your sign will help you understand your personality and the position of your moon at the time of your birth indicates how you respond emotionally in relationships, the connection to your mother, and of course to the Goddess herself.

The Goddess Diana in her Chariot Surrounded by Representations of the Signs of the Zodiac (Lorenzo Costa the Younger). Ritual work can be especially powerful when the moon is in your own moon sign.

| SUN | SELF-EXPRESSION | | The circle symbolizes the feminine principle of the universal force, and the dot at its center is the masculine principle of supreme intelligence, which feeds and stimulates it. |

SUN SELF-EXPRESSION

The circle symbolizes the feminine principle of the universal force, and the dot at its center is the masculine principle of supreme intelligence, which feeds and stimulates it.

MOON EMOTION

The moon represents the soul. It symbolizes the feminine principle, motherhood, pregnancy, the occult, and also dream-time.

MERCURY MENTALITY

This represents the physical life beneath the spirit, with the soul looking upward toward the great consciousness. It is the mind that sets us apart from other animals.

VENUS ATTRACTION

This represents the spirit rising above earthly matters to heal the soul through divine love, the human ability for joy, and creativity.

MARS ASSERTION

The original symbol had a cross; today, it is usually more common to see the arrow. This symbol represents the spirit being motivated into physical action. It signifies humanity's inherent power and energy.

JUPITER EXPANSION

The soul rises above the physical as it yearns for spiritual growth through knowledge and understanding. It symbolizes the human ability for expansion and growth.

SATURN CAUTION

The soul is held firmly in place by physical life; therefore, there is no escape from its karmic tests. It symbolizes humanity's persistence, tenacity, and need for patience.

URANUS ECCENTRICITY

This is the higher expression of Mercury. The initial of Sir William Herschel who discovered Uranus in 1871 stands over the sacred circle, symbolizing exploration and technical development. This signifies that humanity must learn from insight, innovation, and self-control, how to make use of this life for the higher good.

NEPTUNE COMPASSION

This is the higher expression of Venus. The soul is pierced by the physical plane. It symbolizes humanity's aspiration to divine love and completeness.

PLUTO COMPULSION

This is the higher expression of Mars. The soul is the bridge between the spiritual and the physical, and guides the individual toward the higher aspects of loving compassion. Humanity must undergo transformation in order to rise into higher consciousness.

When two people meet and their moons are in the same sign—preferably conjunct (within a few degrees of each other)—it is said to symbolize a meeting of soulmates. You can do especially empowering ritual work when the moon is passing through your moon sign.

PROGRESSED MOON CYCLE

The progression of the moon creates the sacred seven-year life cycle. It passes through each of the 12 zodiac signs every two and a half years, highlighting and enhancing the different characteristics of the sign. These begin to fade as the moon moves into the next sign. This is why many relationships and business ventures will tend either to collapse or go through a considerably testing time around the three-year mark.

The moon's energy turns the tides of life, just as it turns the oceans' tides. The progressed moon takes 28 years to complete the full cycle of the zodiac, and this is the reason why the ages of 28, 46, and 74 are turning-points—the moon has made a complete cycle around the individual's personal astrological chart. Furthermore, every seven years the progressed moon is one-quarter through a complete cycle. When the moon is at right angles to its natal placement it is in a very powerful aspect in astrological terms. These two right-angle positions (ages of 7, 35, and 63, and 21, 49, and 77) create challenges. But when the

The Moon Accompanies Voyage of Sailors—Cancer (*De Sphaera manuscript*). *With its control over the ocean tides, it is not surprising that the moon also influences the turning points in our lives.*

moon is opposite or conjunct with its natal placement (ages 14, 42, and 70, and 28, 56, and 84), new opportunities are often presented, which can lead to radical life changes. No one is exempt from these influences and it is comforting to know that the Goddess allows us more than one chance to put things right.

Part Three

SPELLS, RITUALS, AND CEREMONIES

CHAPTER 9

A WITCH'S ACCOUTREMENTS

A ritual can be as simple or as complex as you wish to make it. Some people like to create an exotic atmosphere by using robes, mantras, swinging incense burners, swords, wands, cauldrons, and so on. But this is not absolutely necessary; it is equally valid to keep your ceremony as simple as possible. Always choose a style that is right for you.

However, for most witches the elemental panoply is an intrinsic part of their work, so even if it is not appropriate for you to use all the witch's accoutrements in your ceremonies, it is important to understand their magical significance. Choose whatever you feel is appropriate, but also try to experiment with different accoutrements—you never know what effect they may have on your ritual.

The Witches' Ride (Otto Goetze).
*The witch's broom had its origins in
sexual superstition. It also symbolizes
the cleansing of negative energy.*

THE BROOM

This may be an optional extra, but it is a lovely one. Just as you need to cleanse yourself, you also need to cleanse the room or outdoor area where you want to work. The broom, or besom, as it is traditionally known, was used to sweep away negative energy from all four corners, and to clear the space within the magic circle. Its shaft is usually made from the ash tree because of its protective qualities. Its brush is made from birch twigs, which offer protection and purification, and is traditionally bound by a young branch from the willow, to instil healing, and love. The willow also governs moon magic.

Fairly innocuous you may think—however, to a witch her besom holds deep sexual significance. The shaft is the male aspect; the broom or bush is the female aspect. In some countries it was considered highly inappropriate for an unmarried girl to step over the broom because it foretold she would be pregnant before becoming a wife. However, when a couple "jumped the besom" as part of their handfasting wedding ceremony, it signified a commonlaw commitment for both parties. This delightful practice is still part of witches' marriage rites today.

The Sorceress *(Lucien Levy-Dhurmer). Darkly mysterious and a spiritual link with the unseen dimension, the black cat has always been closely associated with witches and their magic art.*

The Witch Had Just Made a New Spell! (*Doreen Baxter, illustration from* New Fairy Tales). *Because her special powers were misunderstood, the fairy tale "wicked witch" was shunned by the uninitiated.*

THE WAND

All witches have wands. But why, you may ask. Well, the wand is the representation of air and is used to harness and channel the energy of the spell in whatever direction is needed. The magical quality of each wand differs depending on the wood used for the shaft. Elder and hazel are most commonly used because of their all-purpose magical attributes. For fertility rites, however, it is best to make a wand from oak wood and attach an acorn to the top. The acorn possesses extremely potent fertility magic. Some witches and magicians use staffs (think of, Gandalf in *The Lord of the Rings*), which are also made from appropriate magical trees. Wands and staffs belong to the salamanders of the south.

THE ATHEME, OR SWORD

The atheme is an intensely personal possession that is usually handmade to fit the height of its owner. Ideally, the hilt should come just a little above the solar plexus—the power source of the body. Most witches impregnate their atheme with potent power symbols and secret incantations written in magical alphabets. Traditionally, the handle is made of a black wood to represent the dark moon, while the blade is a silvery steel to signify the full moon. It is used to draw the sacred circle either on the ground or in the air, to summon up the four directions, and to invoke the power of the God and Goddess. In addition to his or her sword, a witch will also possess a much smaller knife that is used exclusively to cut herbs, plants, and flowers for culinary, medicinal, and magical purposes. Both the atheme and the knife belong to the sylphs of the east.

THE CAULDRON

Sadly these days, the lovely old black cast-iron belly-pot on three legs is very rare. Nevertheless, its magical significance is very potent. The three legs represent the triple vision of the Goddess, and its belly is the womb in which special herbal concoctions are mixed and made. In magical terms therefore, the cauldron represents the essence of Mother Nature. The Celtic goddess of the cauldron is Cerridwen who, it is said, set about brewing a potion within her original vessel that could provide universal knowledge. She later became the mother of Taliesin, the Celtic bard

A Visit to the Witch (*Edward Frederick Brewtnall, detail*).
*The witch's black cauldron, generally used for healing
purposes, was more often associated with evil intent.*

who was supposedly the father of Merlin in the Arthurian legends. The cauldron has been very much linked with this Arthurian legend, but as the symbolic form of the grail or chalice. The cauldron, grail, and the chalice belong to the undines of the west.

THE PENTACLE

The "wizard's foot" is the five-pointed star that represents the five senses of man. This is often worn as a protection against negative energies, and sometimes is drawn out within the sacred circle. There are different ways of drawing the pentacle in the air to invoke specific archangels:

URIEL—NORTH DIRECTION

GABRIEL—WEST DIRECTION

RAPHAEL—EAST DIRECTION

MICHAIEL—SOUTH DIRECTION

AZRIEL—CENTRE (ETHER)

When you want to banish something, turn to the north and draw a pentacle nine times either in the air or on a piece of paper, stating what it is you wish to be rid of. The pentacle belongs to the gnomes of the north. The wand, chalice, sword, and pentacle can be symbolized by the aces from the tarot pack, which you place at the appropriate direction.

THE GRIMOIRE,
OR THE BOOK OF SHADOWS

The Crafts are known as the Oral Arts because their secrets have been passed down by word of mouth from generation to generation. This came about because most practitioners were either illiterate or terrified of being discovered by the Inquisition, originally established in Europe in 1233. Those who did write down their findings were forced to disguise them thoroughly and hide them in the most secret of places.

Grimoires, as a witch's book of spells is known (probably meaning dark night, *grim/noir*), were written mainly in Medieval times; however, their sources were far more ancient, the *Key of Solomon* and the *Lesser Key of Solomon* being the most famous. These incredible tomes are attributed to King Solomon himself, who, according to biblical records, was an extremely accomplished magus capable of all manner of incredible feats

and manifestations. The grimoire is also a witch's personal handwritten notebook giving details on healing recipes, results of spells, incantations, etc. Its title "Book of Shadows" reflects the concept that this world is just a mirror of the other life that lies beyond the veil, teaming with spirits, devas, sprites, and angels, and all sorts of magical dreams, visions, and adventures.

I recommend that you start your own grimoire as soon as possible, especially if you wish to incorporate magic ritual as an ongoing part of your life. You can also use it as a diary to note the dates and effects of your rituals, and to record your dream-time. When you open up to this other side, your dreams often change quite dramatically, and sometimes you can receive profound teachings through them. Make sure you use a special pen and appropriately colored ink. This is preferable to a disposable ballpoint pen, which is considered to be less environmentally friendly.

CHAPTER 10

HOW TO MAKE THE
MAGIC WORK FOR YOU

PREPARING FOR A RITUAL

When setting up a ritual, always choose a time when you are not going to be disturbed and a location that is safe from interruptions. Remember, rituals are sacred acts and interruptions dissipate energy. If you are working inside, please make sure that your room is ventilated when burning very heavy incenses. These incenses can become overpowering and in rare cases cause illness, so do take good care of yourself.

Witches always prepare themselves thoroughly before they begin their ritual work. It is advisable to bathe and wash your hair. Put seven drops each of lavender, rosemary and thyme oil into the water and add a small cup of salt. Salt has been used as a psychic cleanser and symbol of purity for thousands of years. The oils contain purification and healing properties, and the number seven is symbolic of the higher mind. It is preferable to wear loose-fitting, comfortable clothes made from natural fabrics, such as cotton, wool, or silk. Natural fabrics are important because they are associated with the simplicity of nature. Some people wear a plaited cord made of red, white, and blue strands around their waists; the cord is knotted three times to remind them of the triple vision of the Goddess. (Monks also do this with white rope to symbolize their vow of poverty, chastity, and obedience). Most witches perform rituals barefoot because it makes them feel more in touch with the earth. Others wear open-toed sandals, but choose whatever is appropriate for you. However, I would advise women to wear clothing that celebrates the Goddess within. Remember, as a woman you are her representative on Earth, and it is far better for your work, and your own inner healing, to do

The Necklace (*John William Waterhouse*). *In celebration of the Goddess within, feminine, loose-fitting clothing is most suited to ritual work.*

everything you can to get in touch with your feminine side. If this presents a problem, rather than reacting negatively, you could simply view it as an aspect of your life that needs looking into.

The Damsel of the Sanctuary Grail (*Dante Gabriel Charles Rossetti*). *Symbols are reminders of the greater reality and our own part in it—we need only use those with special meaning and significance for us.*

The Sacred Circle

The circle represents the very essence of life itself, the Great Mother Goddess, fertility, and manifestation, the all and the nothing. The circle has also been used as a symbol of protection in many cultures for thousands of years and therefore plays a very important role in many different types of ceremonial work. It is usually "drawn" clockwise,

Castlerigg Stone Circle near Keswick
(*James Baker Pyne*). *Stone circles bear witness to ancient connections with the sacred, natural law and the importance of ritual ceremony.*

in the direction of the sun (called going *deosil*), either in the air with an atheme, wand, or hand, or on the ground with chalk. All those taking part in the ritual stay within this circle, and no one should step out of it until the work is complete. It is unwound at the end by walking *widdershins*, the counterclockwise direction of the moon. The sacred circle is traditionally nine feet (2.7 meters) in diameter, which evokes the power of Mars and the nine orders of the angels, and the elemental panoply is placed on the four cardinal directions.

You do not need to create such a huge circle if this appears too daunting. You can create a small circle on your altar, either with the tarot card aces, crystals, much smaller elemental symbols, or with 12 hag stones. These are ordinary stones or pebbles with natural holes made by the elements. They earned the name "hag stones" in Medieval times because they were worn as a protection against witches. The 12 signifies the Great Wheel of Life as described on page 65.

It is important to bear in mind that all these symbols are merely reminders that you are part of the great scheme of things. Be careful not to fall into the trap of giving your power away to them. Many people do not use symbols at all, preferring instead just to meditate with a single candle and a little incense.

Altars

Altars can be created anywhere—as a permanent sacred shrine or as a tool for magical work. Many people from various religious persuasions have special holy places in the home where they spend a little time each day in reflection. Normally, altars are decorated with crystals, flowers, candles, and special personal tokens such as photographs of living avatars, such as Mother Meera or Sai Baba, or religious icons, such as Christ, Buddha, Shakti, or the Dalai Lama. In witchcraft, an ideal altar is above a fireplace since the presence of fire is very evocative. However, you can also make your altar on window sills, small tables, or on the floor.

If you use an altar just for ritual work, make sure that you bless and cleanse what you put onto your altar each time you use it and keep any special utensils wrapped up in silk, separate from the things used in your daily life. This is sacred work, and therefore what you use should also be treated with special care.

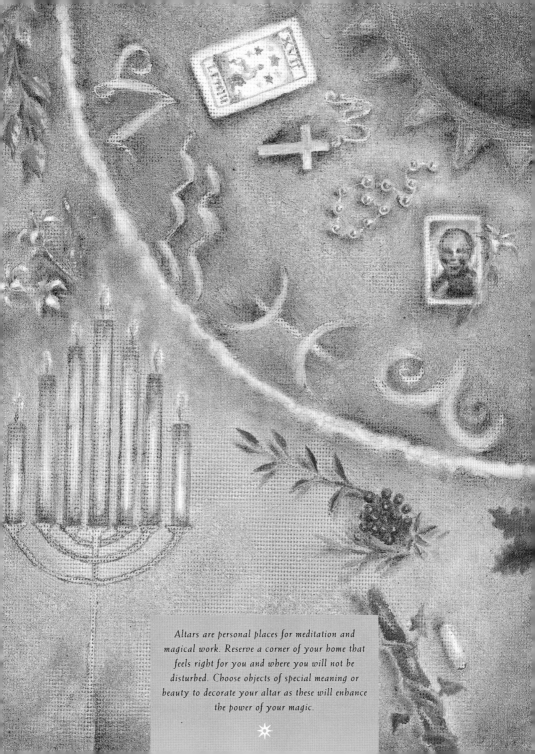

Altars are personal places for meditation and magical work. Reserve a corner of your home that feels right for you and where you will not be disturbed. Choose objects of special meaning or beauty to decorate your altar as these will enhance the power of your magic.

Sunday	Monday	Tuesday	Wednesday	Thursday	Friday	Saturday
Michael	Gabriel	Camael	Raphael	Sachiel	Anaël	Cassiel
name of the 4. Heaven	name of the 1. Heaven	name of the 5 Heaven	name of the 2 Heaven	name of the 6 Heaven	name of the 3 Heaven	No Angels ruling above the 6th Heaven
Machen.	Shamain.	Machon.	Raquie.	Zebul.	Sagun.	

Pages from *The Magus* and a Table Showing
the Seven Days of the Week with their
Governing Angels, Symbols, and Astrological
Signs (*Francis Barrett*).

CHOOSING THE CORRECT DAY OF THE WEEK

The days of the week are important because each is affiliated not only to an astrological sign and magical power but also to a particular god and goddess.

DAY	ASTROLOGICAL SIGN		DEITY	MAGICAL POWER
MONDAY		MOON	*Diana, Roman goddess of the moon*	*Home, fertility, childbirth, women, money*
TUESDAY		MARS	*Tiw, Norse war god*	*Passion, courage, sexual energy, war, men*
WEDNESDAY		MERCURY	*Woden, chief Norse god*	*Communication, education, travel, mental alertness, writing, tricks*
THURSDAY		JUPITER	*Thor, Norse god of thunder, sky, and weather*	*Expansion, wealth, benevolence, politics, law, business, weather*
FRIDAY		VENUS	*Frija, wife of Woden, goddess of sex and love*	*Love, beauty, music, the arts, nature*
SATURDAY		SATURN	*Saturn, Roman god of time*	*Karmic justice, property, inheritance, land and farming*
SUNDAY		SUN	*Sol, the sun god*	*Success, power, healing, ambition, physical prowess, career*

You can call on the power of the relevant god or goddess as part of your invocations, which we will talk about in detail later on. This involves selecting the day, time, and moon phase. For example, if you want to conduct a love spell, you would do it on a Friday night during the waxing phase of the moon; a fertility ritual should be done on a Monday night during the full moon; to change your job, you need to perform a releasing ritual on a Thursday night during the waning phase to make room for a new one to come.

The Mirror of Venus (*Sir Edward Burne-Jones*).
*Study the phases of the moon and let them
be your guide, both in ritual work and in
your everyday life.*

CHOOSING THE CORRECT PHASE OF THE MOON

The phases of the moon play a vital role in selecting which day you should conduct particular types of rituals. Four phases need to be taken into consideration:

DARK MOON

This is when the moon is said to be most mysterious and nebulous; therefore, very few witches conduct rituals at this time. Instead, they use the darkness to look into their hearts to see what they want to draw into their lives once the crescent moon appears.

NEW MOON AND WAXING CRESCENT

The phase between the appearance of the crescent moon and the build-up to the full moon is the time to draw in what you wish to create in your life. This phase of the moon has the power to illuminate your desires.

FULL MOON OR FERTILE MOON

This is the time of fruition and the perfect opportunity to create a special meeting with friends to assess the past month. It is also the time to give thanks for all that has happened and to come to terms with what no longer serves you.

WANING MOON

This is the phase for reducing or banishing spells—for example, spells for leaving a job, losing weight, saying goodbye to an old love affair, ending a feud, moving house.

The Witches *(after Gustav Spangenberg). A time of fruition and assessment, the full moon is the time to let go of old, outmoded habits and whatever is holding you back.*

CANDLES

Most rituals, secular or religious, use candles as a focal point. Fire is illumination and therefore the flame draws to it spirits and angels from beyond the veil. The flame is also used to symbolize the very essence of the divine life force—the spark that lies within us all.

In any ritual work candles play a vital part, particularly their color, because each vibrates to a certain magical quality. The first seven colors listed below are affiliated to the seven chakras or energy centers of the body and to the seven colors of the rainbow. The number of candles you use depends on the ceremony you are conducting, as shown on the following page.

Garlic (Tacuinum Sanitatum). Garlic has since early times been associated with witchcraft and folklore, and its powerful purifying and healing properties are well established in herbal medicine.

CHAKRA	COLOR	MAGICAL QUALITY
1ST	RED	*Passion, sexual energy, strength, courage*
2ND	ORANGE	*Positive thinking, justice, change of circumstances*
3RD	YELLOW	*Creativity, imagination, communication*
4TH	GREEN	*Abundance, fertility, harmony, good luck, the home*
5TH	BLUE	*Healing, truth, inspiration, higher wisdom*
6TH	PURPLE	*Spiritual power, psychic abilities*
7TH	WHITE	*Purity, devotion, peace*
	PINK	*Love and friendship*
	SILVER	*Channeling, clairvoyance, astral energies*
	GOLD	*Prosperity, riches, and money*
	BROWN	*Animal healing*
	BLACK	*Banishing, releasing*

CEREMONY	NUMBER OF CANDLES	MAGICAL POWER
PERSONAL EXPRESSION	1	*Power of the Sun*
MONEY, THE HOME, FERTILITY	2	*Power of the Moon*
LEGAL ISSUES, CREATIVITY	3	*Power of Jupiter*
STABILITY, COMMITMENT	4	*Power of Uranus*
COMMUNICATION, CHANGE	5	*Power of Mercury*
LOVE, HEALTH	6	*Power of Venus*
HEALING, HIGHER WISDOM	7	*Power of Neptune*
ABUNDANCE, CAREER	8	*Power of Saturn*
SEXUAL ENERGY/COURAGE	9	*Power of Mars*
RELEASING SPELLS	3, 5 or 9	

Odd numbers are extremely important in magical work since they stand for creativity, inspiration, and adventure. They expand things and push things forward, literally shifting the course of nature. So these are used when you want to change something in your life.

The even numbers provide form and stability, so use these when you want to make something solid and long-lasting.

OIL, INCENSE, AND HERBAL OFFERINGS

Candle magic can be enhanced by the anointing of certain herbal oils that resonate with the theme of the spell, a custom which is extremely ancient. The aroma helps to raise the vibrations, much like the use of incense. Oil is also a symbol of fire and acts as a messenger of intent carried by the smoke as it spirals upward toward the

heavens. You can make your own by either adding essential oils to a carrier oil, such as grapeseed or almond, or putting fresh leaves in a carrier oil for several weeks.

Likewise, you can incorporate fresh or dried herbs into your ritual by placing them in a bowl of water, scattering them on the earth or throwing them on the fire as a gesture to the Goddess.

Magical herbalism or *wortcunning* as it used to be known, is a truly vast subject. It needs a great deal of study, which I recommend you do if you wish to pursue the Old Crafts in any depth. Invest in a good book (there are several listed in the Further Reading section); in the meantime you can use the chart on the next page as a guideline.

If all this appears too daunting, you could invest in some rosemary oil and a small rosemary tree. This is the witch's fail-safe herb that can be used in all types of magical rituals. It is said to evoke

SPELL	OIL	HERB
LOVE	ROSE OR GERANIUM (6 DROPS)	Basil, apple, dill
LUST	YLANG-YLANG (9 DROPS)	Thyme, parsley
PROSPERITY	BERGAMOT (3 DROPS)	Honeysuckle, ginger
HEALING	ROSEMARY (7 DROPS)	Lavender, fennel
PROTECTION	FRANKINCENSE (5 DROPS)	Bay, orris
LUCK	NUTMEG (5 DROPS)	Orange rind, poppy
BUSINESS	CINNAMON (8 DROPS)	Mint, pine
MONEY	MINT (2 DROPS)	Honeysuckle, nutmeg
SUCCESS	GINGER (9 DROPS)	Lemon balm, clove
PEACE	LAVENDER (7 DROPS)	Gardenia, skullcap
FERTILITY	PATCHOULI (2 DROPS)	Fig, hawthorn

The Fountain of Youth (*Edward Veith*).
What qualities do you most desire? Seek out the
appropriate herbs and oils to help you draw in
the lover of your dreams.

the souls of the Old Ones as well as promoting luck, healing, love, purification, and protection. Frankincense is another great favorite originally used to honor the sun god Ra. It also has the capacity to raise the higher consciousness and promote visions. Its counterpart, myrrh, is dedicated to the goddess Isis and increases the power of any other incenses to which it is added. The male quality of frankincense combined with the female essence of myrrh make these extremely potent oils and incenses. It was not without significance that the three wise men brought gold, frankincense, and myrrh to honor the Christ Child, said to be born on the day of the great sun god Sol.

Lux in Tenebris (*Evelyn de Morgan*). *A sprig of*
hawthorn adds potency to a fertility spell; lavender
aids healing. Tap into the power of the Goddess,
who is the energy behind all natural phenomena.

The Witches in Macbeth (*Alexandre Gabriel Decamps*).
Witches got a bad press in the past, but the concept
of witchcraft is changing slowly to one of positivity,
healing, and enlightenment.

SPELL-CASTING: A FEW CAUTIONARY NOTES

Now that you are in possession of certain important facts and information, you are ready to get on with the fun part of spell-casting! But before we start, I have a few words of caution.

Never seek to invade another's private thoughts or personal space through the use of magic, or manipulate someone against his or her will. This is not using magic wisely. The universal law states that anything you do will reverberate upon you with ten times as much force. As long as you remember that witchcraft is used only to heal and help, you cannot go wrong.

Before you begin to cast spells, it is very important to understand the difference between invocation and evocation. Invocation is when you invite an entity to come into your body, and you act as a channel for its energies. I do not advise this unless you are highly trained in this area, or work with skilled people who can help the process to proceed safely. Evocation is inviting a spirit to "manifest" in your presence, not in physical form, but as an astral experience within the mind's eye. Many witches evoke the protection of archangels, their guides, and the devic realms as they begin their ritual. This is quite simple to do. The method of evocation in the following

"I am Half Sick of Shadows"
said the Lady Of Shalott
(A. John William Waterhouse).
Before beginning ritual work, the
practitioner needs to be in a healthy,
balanced state of mind and body.

spells can be adapted for any spell-casting you choose to do, either with friends or on your own.

In the world of witchcraft, health is linked to state of mind, which is usually exacerbated by a poor or inappropriate diet. If you are physically ill, it is a sign that your soul is ill at ease and is trying to tell you that you have stepped off your rightful path. In fact, the Taoists believe that any form of physical illness means that you are not following your life's true purpose. Illness indicates that you need to stop and reassess everything in your life. The fact that your body has realized this is a big step toward a more positive future for you. However, if you have strayed very far off course, quite a few things in your life will probably need to change in order for you to get back on track. So before you attempt to cast a spell, it is a good idea to take the time to find out about your body and what is right and wrong for it. Don't underestimate the challenge of making changes to your life, and ensure you have as much support as you need.

Bearing this in mind, make sure you have paper and colored pens available since spell-casting usually involves writing down what you wish to release as well as what you wish to manifest. You should also have any appropriate oils and herbs at the ready (see page 112).

CHAPTER 11

HEALING SPELLS

INNER-HEALING JOURNEY

You may want to record the following journey of inner healing onto an audio tape to play during the ritual, or you can just allow your own inner journey to develop at its own pace.

This ritual comes under the auspices of the sun; therefore, Sunday is the day to choose for your healing journey. Since you want to draw in healing, it should be conducted during the waxing phase of the moon. This particular spell is for your own inner healing, which is always the first place to start. It can be adapted to help other people and animals through absent healing. In these cases place their photographs or their names on your altar.

◖ Place your altar facing north (the direction of manifestation) or wherever it feels most comfortable. Decorate it with fresh flowers, which automatically raise the vibration of healing through their color and aroma. Place one blue candle on each of the four directions and another

The Creation of the Sun and Moon (detail from stained-glass window). A Sunday when the moon is waxing is ideal for an inner healing ritual.

three blue candles on your altar, making a total of seven. Place appropriate symbols in the four directions and light your incense.

◖ Turn to the east, and welcome the sylphs, the airy ones, into your circle. Ask for their guidance, protection, and illumination, then light the candle.

◖ Turn to the south and welcome the salamanders, the fiery ones, into your circle and ask for their guidance, protection, and inspiration, then light the candle.

◖ Turn to the west and welcome the undines, the watery ones, into your circle. Ask for their guidance, protection, and emotional clarity, then light the candle.

◖ Finally, turn to the north and welcome the gnomes, the earthy ones, into your circle. Ask for their guidance, protection, and abundance, then light the candle.

The healing touch can channel energy where it is needed. When asking for absent healing call on the elemental spirits and ask for guidance.

Healing takes place in an atmosphere of peace, compassion, and trust. We can all learn to channel the cosmic energies that surround us, combining these with the amazing power of our own thoughts and imagination.

You should ask for the blessings and protection of the Goddess, and if you wish you can call her by a name that resonates best with you, for example, Isis, Diana or Demeter. Light the remaining three candles. You can also evoke the powers of the archangels.

Close your eyes and become aware of your body. What does it feel

Plants and trees hold many magic, healing secrets still to be discovered. Simple herbs and essences play an important part in witchcraft and offer a gentle alternative to modern medicines.

like to be within it? Is it comfortable and nurturing, or does it feel uncomfortable and ill at ease? Do you like your body? Just allow any thoughts to float through your mind, acknowledge them, and then release any negative emotions by breathing through your mouth. Allow your body to relax, and remember that you have evoked the power of the elemental spirits and the Goddess to help you during this inner journey.

Call the Goddess to you and give her your worries and discomforts. She will take them away so that you can free yourself to allow the magic of the elements to appear to you. Take a few moments to feel her power and her love. She is unconditional with her love and will accept you just the way you are, because she knows that you are on a fantastic journey of discovery. Where you are right now is exactly where you are meant to be. If you feel emotions coming up, allow your tears to flow, they are very often the key to our inner healing.

Allow the Goddess to stand beside you, and then permit her to lead you into a magnificent garden that is full of color and vibration. Let this come alive within you. Now look at the sky and call upon the sylphs of the air that provide you with the very breath of life. Without air we cannot live upon this planet.

The sylphs bring you a gift of illumination that you dearly need to enhance your mind and your intellect. Receive this knowledge and give thanks for it. Now turn around to see a great fire and call upon the salamanders. Fire is the source of our inspiration and courage. It warms our bodies and souls and fuels our gifts of creativity. The salamanders bear a gift of knowledge that you dearly need to help you to attune to your life's purpose. Receive this knowledge and give thanks for it.

Now you see a body of water. See the wind playing with the surface of the water and how, beneath the surface, it is teaming with life. See how important clear, clean water is for your own welfare. The water undines bear you a gift of knowledge that you dearly need for your heart-healing. Receive this knowledge and give thanks.

Finally, take your attention to the earth itself. See how it provides you with everything you could possibly wish for. The gnomes come to you with a gift of knowledge that you dearly need

Water Nymphs *(Sidney Meteyard)*. In a ritual of inner healing, the water undines will cleanse
your body, mind, and soul, and bring you the special personal knowledge you need.

The God Bacchus and Goddess Ar adne
(*Luca Giordano*). *At the end of your inner-healing
ritual, give thanks to the spirits and take time to
note any changes that have occurred.*

to enhance your physical health and welfare. Receive this knowledge and give thanks.

The sylph spirit takes you soaring into the realm of air. Feel its purity cleansing away any blockages within your mind. Pay homage to it and when you are done, say farewell to the sylph.

Now the salamander spirit takes you deep into its fiery realm. Allow the fire to burn away any disease you may be carrying in your body. Pay homage to it and when you are done, say farewell to the salamander.

The undine spirit is ready

Spirit of the Night (*John Atkinson Grimshaw*). *During your healing ritual, call on the air spirits to bring you the illumination you need.*

to take you far into its watery domain. Allow the crystal clear water to wash every part of your body, mind, and soul. Pay homage to it and when you are done, say farewell to the undine.

Finally, the gnome spirit leads you into the depth of the earth kingdom. Feel the power of the earth providing you with all the strength and prowess that you need. Pay homage to it and then say farewell to the gnome.

The Goddess appears again at your side. Pay homage to her power and wisdom. Then say your farewell and allow her to enter into your heart, for this is where she wishes to reside. Now begin to feel yourself inside your body once more. Notice if anything has changed. Take a few deep breaths and open your eyes.

Take some time to make notes on what has happened during your inner-healing journey. Has anything come to mind that you know you need to release? Make a list of these things and keep this list until the waning phase of the moon when you can conduct a special releasing ceremony (see page 130). This is a perfect time to scatter your herbs into a bowl of water as a mark of respect to the Goddess, and also to anoint yourself with the healing oil either on your forehead or directly onto your heart. This should be made up of seven drops of lavender essential oil into a carrier oil such as grapeseed or almond.

If there are friends to whom you would like to send healing thoughts, do so now. Pick up their photographs or name them and imagine a white light beaming into their hearts. It is also a wonderful gesture to send healing thoughts to the planet itself, to the four elements and all the creatures of the earth.

The Goddess plays a vital role in your inner-healing ritual. She will help you to release both physical and emotional worries.

If you so wish, you can say the following incantation seven times:

Healing light, come swift and fast
Straight to the hearts of man and beast.
Let peace and love pervade.
All is well. Blessed be.

Some people like to chant for a few minutes to conclude their ceremony. The mantra "Hu," for example, is used by many Buddhists and Sufis. This has the effect of opening up the heart and allowing the flow of the universal love to pulsate within the body. "Hu" is the ancient love song

Ariadne in Naxos (*George Frederick Watts*). *As inner healing begins, the Goddess will appear beside you to take away your fears and pain and lead you on a voyage of discovery.*

to God and comes from an ancient word for God. Chanting this love song opens us up to seek the wisdom and power that resides deep within us.

It is best to allow your candles to burn down completely, so once you feel complete, make sure they burn down safely. Scatter the herbs and water on the ground outside, or into a plant pot, and give thanks to the Goddess as you do so.

HEALING POPPETS

For absent healing you can also make what is known in the trade as a poppet. This is a special blue felt doll which is made in the shape of a person or animal. While you are cutting out the shape, send healing thoughts to the person or animal to be healed. It is the concentration that counts. Now embroider or draw healing symbols onto the heart of the poppet and then stuff it with herbs such as lavender, bay, thyme, rosemary, and nettle. If possible, include a piece of the person's hair or fingernail. As you are making the poppet, recite the following healing mantra seven times:

I name this poppet ...... [name of person/animal].
Let .... be well,
Let .... be whole.
Healing come fast and true.
.... is indeed well. Blessed be.

Place your poppet on your altar and put some fresh blue flowers beside it. Leave it there for a whole cycle of the moon. As it passes into the waning phase, you should light seven candles and then bury the poppet in the earth—literally burying the disease.

Poppets can be used for all manner of magic. For example, if you want to draw a partner to you, make two poppets, one male (using blue material) and one female (using pink material) on a Friday night in the waxing phase of the moon. Light six pink candles and then fill the poppets with a mixture of basil, chamomile, dill, and orange peel to which three drops of geranium oil has been added. Recite the following mantra three times:

The Valley of Shadows *(Evelyn de Morgan).*
In attuning ourselves to the natural order of the
cosmos and the greater scheme of things, we are no
longer weighed down by temporary cares.

Love come to
my bidding,
Let it be strong and true.
I open my heart to
receive it,
I open my
eyes to see it,
I open my
ears to hear it,
I open my
arms to hold it.
So mote it be.

Bind the two poppets face to face with green cord that is knotted six times. Present the entwined pair to the four elemental spirits, and finally to the Goddess for her benediction. Place them on your altar for six days and nights, then wrap them in a white cloth and put them in a safe place where they will never be unbound.

Alternatively, if you just want to draw in a passing love affair, make your two poppets on a Tuesday night (governed by Mars, God of Lust) and keep them bound until your affair has run its course and you have parted company.

*"Mote it be" is a witch's blessing akin to "Amen."

Traditional herbs for spells, medicines, and healing poppets from The Physic Garden.

Full Moon behind Cirrus Cloud, from Roundhay Castle (*John Atkinson Grimshaw*). *When you have made a healing poppet, leave it on your altar for a full cycle of the moon.*

Afterwards, scatter the herbs to the wind, and burn the poppet to release you both from any psychic or karmic ties. But remember to take responsibility for what you create in your life. If you use magic to draw someone in, be prepared for the unexpected. And do be honest with new lovers. You don't necessarily have to confess to drawing them in by magic, but tell them if you are not interested in a committed relationship, merely looking for some fun with someone nice. Otherwise that old universal law of mistakes returning to you with ten times as much force will catch you when you least expect it.

In the Morning of the World (*George Percy Jacomb-Hood*). *Make your love spells with honesty and care—love will flourish best in an atmosphere of compassion, generosity, and acceptance.*

CHAPTER 12

LOVE SPELLS

The Vision of Endymion (*Sir Edward John Poynter*). *Concentrate in detail on your ideal lover and send your thoughts out to the universe, so that the dream can become reality.*

This is the section that most people flick to first because everyone wants to find their own true love! And yes, he or she can be extremely elusive! But why, when we all, men and women alike, want love so desperately? After many years of searching for the answer, I have come to the conclusion that the answer is down to karmic fate. Some of us are meant to experience true love with just one person, while others have to learn about the course of love through many partnerships, involving a certain amount of heartbreak interspersed with the heady heights of passion and mayhem that accompany the state of being "in love." In the process, we are constantly shown the state of our own hearts, and the healing we still need to undergo in order to find peace within a loving relationship. So can magic help or speed up this process? I believe that when we open our hearts to the Goddess, things do start to happen that can be truly magical. But we cannot come into the state of loving someone else fully until we are comfortable with ourselves. Negative thoughts get in the way, and all too often our feelings of unworthiness kill the seed before it has a chance to take root. Men are no different from women in this respect. They just hide it a bit better, that's all.

So if you want to draw love into your life, you need to do a little inward searching first. Since another law of the universe is that like attracts like, it is important to ask yourself if now is really the right moment to attract someone who will

The Passing of Venus (Sir Edward Burne-Jones). Wait for the waxing phase of the moon and call upon the power of Venus, Goddess of Love, to empower your love spell.

unquestionably be in the same mutual and spiritual space as yourself. If in your present state of being you are loving, generous, and ready to commit without seeking to own, then the principle of "like attracts like" will work in your favor. But if you are desperately lonely and fearful of abandonment, rejection, humiliation, and betrayal, then trouble lies ahead. Desperation draws in desperation. And our worst fears are always brought to light through intimate relationships. You must deal with these issues if you want to attract a lasting relationship that is nurturing, kind, and gentle.

Healing rituals are a tremendous help in clearing your path, and as this happens you will automatically draw to you different lovers and friends who will support you along your way.

In this respect, the magic does indeed work, and you may well feel that it is more appropriate at the present time to stay with your healing. However, if you feel that now is the time to call in that special person, the following ritual should do the trick!

A LOVE SPELL

All love spells should be conducted on Friday nights, in order to fall under the auspices of Venus, Goddess of Love. They should also be conducted during the waxing phase of the moon.

Draw a really luxurious bath, into which you pour six drops of geranium oil, six drops of lavender oil, and six drops of ylang-ylang:

$3 \times 6 = 18; 1 + 8 = 9; 9$ is the number
of Mars and the male principle.

Scatter rose petals on the water, light a pink candle, and as you enter the water evoke the power of Venus or Aphrodite into your heart. Recite the following mantra six times:

du Roy et de la Royne et en mena yseult faysant
moult grant Joye C mess trista et yseult la Roye
beurent ensemble le bruuage Amoureup.

Tristan and Isolde Drink the Love Potion (*Medieval manuscript*).
Creating a love spell is powerful, so beware of the consequences!

This water is to heal my heart,
This flame is to light my fire,
This steam is to inspire my thoughts,
These petals are to nurture my body.
All is well. Blessed be.

Take plenty of time to really enjoy your cleansing ritual, then dress in a comfortable white robe and tie a pink cord that has been knotted six times around your waist.

Draw out your sacred circle, and place your altar facing north—the place of manifestation. Place four pink candles on the four directions and two pink candles on your altar. Decorate your altar with roses and stones such as red jasper (since this is the stone of love and passion), pink tourmaline, amethyst, or kunzite (a very beautiful and powerful love stone). Light your candles and as you do so say the following mantra:

Love I bid thee come.
Come, carried by
the four winds,
Come on the tides
of the oceans,
Come in the flaming light,
Come riding across the earth,
Come in the arms of the
Goddess. Love I bid thee come.
All is well. Blessed be.

Caritas *(Sir Edward Burne-Jones). Remember to state exactly what you want (and don't want) in a relationship. If you're not too keen on children, don't forget to mention this fact!*

Light some special love incense—preferably loose-grain incense that can be burnt on a piece of charcoal in a heat-proof dish. (The incense and charcoal pieces can be bought in any New Age shop.) Now take a piece of paper, some colored pens and inks, and write or sketch the kind of relationship you want to draw into your life. You could also make a collage from newspaper headlines and magazine pictures. Spend some time over it, because it is through dedicated concentration that the doorway into the universal consciousness opens up. Once the universe knows what you want, it can begin to create the circumstances to manifest it. Remember to list what is really important to you: for example, someone who is free from emotional commitments, relative in age, healthy, plays tennis, likes cats, and so on. These details are important, for it is quite possible to draw in an unsuitable situation—for instance, someone who is married, too old, has a dependent relationship with parents or hates cats! None of these scenarios would bode well for a balanced, harmonious partnership, though the universe sometimes appears to have an extraordinary sense of humor whereby you receive exactly what you forgot to say you didn't want!

Once you are happy with what you have done, spend a little time just meditating on your picture. Close your eyes and relax. Allow your thoughts to drift through your mind until it begins to clear. Then ask the Goddess for a symbol of love to come into your mind. This could happen as a feeling, as a sense, or as a vision. If nothing appears immediately, don't despair, the symbol may appear in your dreams, or you could experience a realization later, while going about your daily business. If you do receive something, draw it or write it down immediately. This is now your love talisman, which you need to place with your other drawing. Place it into a special spell box (which you can buy or make for yourself), put it on your altar, and surround it with sprigs of fresh rosemary and a small basil plant. Leave it for the whole cycle of the moon. During this time you can add other love tokens if you so wish. A partner could well manifest before the cycle of the moon is complete. If so, make sure you hold a special ritual of thanksgiving to the Goddess, either alone or with your new partner. However, if someone has not appeared and this is

Call upon Venus to send you a symbol of love. The Goddess will be working behind the scenes on your behalf.

beginning to consume your mind, it is important to conduct a "releasing" ceremony. This is not about letting go of any hope of drawing in a partner, rather it is a gesture of surrender to the Great Force. It is very difficult for the Great Force to work on your behalf if you are continually attempting to manipulate situations through illusory imaginings.

On a Friday night, light one silver and one gold or yellow candle, evoke the Goddess and then take out your first drawing. Call in the four directions, and offer your drawing to each direction in turn while you recite an incantation such as the following:

Love come to my bidding.
Come from the east,
Come from the south,
Come from the west,
Come from the north,
Come in the arms of the Goddess.
Love come to my bidding.
All is well. Blessed be.

Light some frankincense and myrrh, and hold a piece of rose quartz in your left hand.

Now close your eyes and imagine you are drawing the sacred circle in white light. Within the circle you should draw a large pentacle, the points of which touch the edge of the circle. As you take your place in the center of the circle you see to the east a doorway appearing. Place your hand on your heart and call in your future partner through the doorway.

Herbs need to be gathered at specific times for their "active principle" to be at its most potent.

Welcome Footsteps (*Sir Lawrence Alma-Tadema*). *Have patience and put your trust in the power of the universal consciousness. When the time is right, your lover will come into your life.*

Francesca da Rimini (*William Dyce*). *When you surrender your feelings of loneliness to the Goddess of Love and ask for her help, miracles can soon start to happen.*

Precious stones are important to many magic spells and healing rituals. Red jasper, pink tourmaline, amethyst, and rose quartz provide some of the beautiful and empowering elements of love spells.

☽ Watch what happens.

☽ How is he/she dressed?

☽ What is his/her attitude?

☽ Invite him/her to sit facing you.

☽ Place your hand on his/her heart and put his/her hand on your heart. Feel the energy building between you.

☽ Tell him/her why you have called him/her.

☽ When you feel complete, take him/her to the direction of the north where a doorway has opened. Unconditionally, allow him/her to walk away from you through the doorway.

☽ As he/she walks away, say the following incantation:

> *Love I bid thee go free.*
> *For when the time is right,*
> *You will come back to me.*
> *All is well. Blessed be.*

Return to the center of the pentacle and pay homage to the Goddess and the Great Force. They have your best interests at heart, so surrender your needs and loneliness to them. When the time is right, rest assured, your partner will come.

Leave the pentacle through the door of the west, the place of dreams. Know that at any time you can return to this place of serenity from the doorway of the east. Open your eyes and take time to look at your drawing again. Once you feel complete, offer it to the fire of the south, the place of innocence. Watch it burn and as it does so, repeat the incantation:

> *Love, I bid thee go free.*
> *For when the time is right,*
> *You will come back to me.*
> *All is well. Blessed be.*

Now take your rose quartz and bury it in the ground along with the ashes—if possible under an apple tree. If you do not have a garden, bury it in a pot of basil. Every time you feel lonely or desolate, just call the Goddess to you and "hand up" these feelings to her. This does

The Lady of Shalott *(John William Waterhouse).*
If you just want some fun and relaxation, work your
magic during the full moon before casting your love
spell into a moving stream.

take a certain amount of self-discipline and a willingness to surrender your heart. Nevertheless, I can absolutely assure you that things will rapidly begin to change in all sorts of miraculous ways when you remember to do this on a regular basis.

CALLING A LOVER

Perhaps you know you are not ready for a life partner, but would like to find someone for a little fun and relaxation to while away the long winter nights, or to frolic with during those warm balmy summer evenings. If so, this ritual could provide exactly what you need. It should be done over the three days of the full moon, that is, the day before, the day of, and the day after the full moon. Dress yourself in red underwear if possible, because this is the color of sexual passion. Bind together mint, rosemary, parsley, a cinnamon stick and dill with a red cord knotted nine times and arrange it on your altar. Score two red candles with your initials on one side and the words "my lover" on the other. (Remember, you must never ask for a specific person.) Place the candles on your altar at opposite ends and as you light them say the

following incantation nine times:

> *I call to you*
> *across the void,*
> *Come in freedom*
> *and come for fun!*
> *Blessed be.*

Light some incense and then move the candles a little nearer each other. Visualize yourself meeting a lover who is the perfect person for you. After one hour extinguish the flames. Never blow candles out; it is said that this blows away the magic.

The following night, which will be that of the full moon, repeat the process again, moving the candles a little nearer to each other.

On the third night, repeat the spell once more, move the candles so that they touch each other, and allow them to burn down together completely. Then collect the burnt incense, candle stubs, and herbs and put them into a pouch made of red felt or silk upon which you have painted or embroidered the entwined glyphs of Mars and Venus. Take the pouch to a moving river, stream, pond, or ocean and as you cast it into the waters call on the Goddess Aphrodite to provide for you. She is the Goddess of Love and Passion. Now walk away without looking back. This is an important part of the ritual because it represents the process of letting go of the outcome. Be prepared for people to become very attracted to you, but make sure you do not take advantage of them. Always be honest, and no harm can come to any of you.

At Aphrodite's Cradle (*Sir Lawrence Alma-Tadema*). *Ask the Goddess Aphrodite to bring love and passion into your life. The sea—Aphrodite's birthplace—gives powerful healing to mind and body.*

CHAPTER 13

TRADITIONAL SPELLS AND RITUALS

DRAWING YOUR LIFE'S
PURPOSE TO YOU

This is predominantly a fire spell, so it should either be conducted in front of a fire in the grate or outdoors near a bonfire. If neither are possible, you should sit in the south position, the realm of fire and inspiration.

Since you want to draw information to you, do this ritual during the waxing phase of the moon, on a Wednesday, since this is the day for communication. Decorate your altar with yellow flowers—yellow being the color of creativity— and light five yellow candles—one on each direction, and one in the center of your altar. Set up your ritual as outlined in the healing spell (see page 116), evoke the elemental spirits and your Goddess.

To help with your concentration, try holding a power in your hand—a piece of amber to bring ancient knowledge to you, aventurine to enhance imagination, or sodalite to help unite logic with the spirit.

Sit quietly for a few moments and breathe deeply. Allow any tension that you may still be harboring to leave through your exhalations. Stare deep into the fire or flame of your candle, and allow it to take you far inside yourself. Recite the following mantra five times:

Choose runic symbols that feel pleasing and personally significant to you. Incorporate them into the ritual.

*Spirit of the fire
speak to me.
Show me my way
through flame,
Show me my way
through water,
Show me my way
through earth,
Show me my way
through air.
I draw to me the
vision of my path,
Which now manifests
in love and peace.*

Allow your mind to quiet and receive. Do not be concerned if nothing happens straight away. Just allow the silence to do its work. You may find yourself remembering childhood dreams and ambitions, or your thoughts may drift toward something in the very back of your mind. Perhaps you will receive nothing except the sense of peace that comes from giving yourself time to really consider your life's path.

Take a piece of paper and write down anything that comes to you, and decorate it with runic and astrological symbols that appeal to you (see pages 84

"Drawing your life's purpose to you" is a fire spell. Light candles on your altar, relax, breathe deeply, and allow your mind to grow quiet and the silence to do its work. Open yourself to whatever visions or buried memories may appear.

and 93). Then write your mantra five times. Pass the piece of paper over the four elemental flames, calling in each devic entity to bless and protect it. Now lay it on your altar surrounded by the flowers. Place your crystals on it and any other image you feel is appropriate. Leave it there until the full moon.

On the full moon, light five yellow candles and evoke the energies of the Goddess. Take your paper and offer it to the flames, saying the following mantra five times as the paper burns:

Light of the moon, shine your truth.
Show me my way, show me my path.
So mote it be.

Once you feel complete, scatter the ashes into the wind (preferably when it is blowing in a southerly direction) and allow the heavens to lead

Day *(Edward Robert Hughes). If you want to discover your life's destiny, conduct a ritual, calling upon the Goddess and the spirits to give you an insight to what lies ahead.*

you toward your destiny. This may unfold in all sorts of unusual ways, so make a note in your grimoire of such things as synchronistic meetings, strange coincidences, or powerful prophetic dreams. Once you are willing to find your true destiny, the angelic forces literally dance for joy.

FERTILITY RITUAL

Fertility rituals are best conducted during the week before the full moon. Arrange on the left-hand side of your altar all the juicy female foods you can find—melons, figs, peaches, dates—and on the right, all the male foods—bananas, carrots, nuts, and olives. Scatter rice among the two piles. In the center place three uncooked eggs on a bed of oak leaves. Paint the glyph of the moon on

Prepare your altar with female and male fruits and call on the Goddess of Fertility before lighting a silver and a gold candle in honor of the feminine and masculine elements.

the left egg, the glyph of the sun on the right one, and the glyph of Jupiter on the center one. Place a silver candle among your female fruit, and a gold candle among your male fruit.

Next, arrange the seven chakra candles (see page 110) in a circle around the fruit and eggs. This symbolizes the womb. Anoint each candle with two drops of patchouli oil. As you light the candles, one by one, evoke the Goddess of Fertility in the guise of Isis, Demeter, Ceres, or with whomever you feel an affinity. Call upon her to help you to realize your dream of creation. Now light your silver candle in honor of the feminine, and the gold candle in honor of the masculine. Without the union of these two elements, nature cannot provide. Allow yourself plenty of time to visualize what you are wishing

to accomplish, and if this is to conceive a child, call upon the spirit of the child to appear to you. When you feel complete, extinguish the candles with your fingers or a candle snuffer.

Repeat this process for seven days and seven nights, the final night being that of the full moon. Allow the candles to burn down completely. Place all the fruit in a red bag and tie with green cord that is knotted twice. Place the three eggs and the oak leaves in a blue bag tied with green cord that is knotted three times. Tie these two bags together and leave them on your altar until the

The Newborn Child *(Georges de la Tour).*
Miracles can happen. The power of your own
wishes, combined with the mysterious forces of the
universe, can help you achieve your dream.

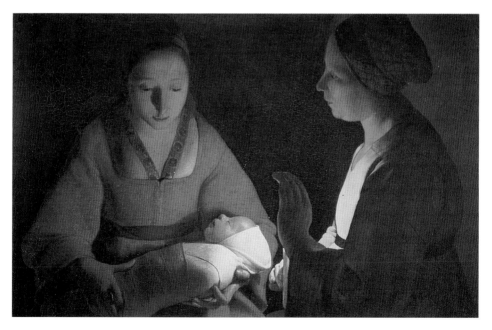

A Bacchant Carrying a Cherub *(Roman fresco). Ask that your future child's spirit appears to you. When the moon is full, light five yellow candles and call upon the Goddess.*

first Monday after the full moon. Take the bags to the base of an oak tree, dig a deep hole and bury the bags. Dedicate your creation to your Goddess, and ask her to pour her blessing of fertility onto you. Repeat your dedication three times. Now ask the oak tree for its blessing and protection. The oak holds very powerful fertility powers. When you have completed this part of the ritual, take three acorns from the oak, or three leaves if acorns are out of season. Give thanks. Walk away without looking back, and place the acorns or leaves in a special pouch on your altar.

If you feel this ritual is a little complex, just light two silver candles, evoke the Goddess, and ask for her help and blessing. Whatever you choose to do, remember it is

Call upon the power and abundance of the oak tree and ask for its blessing and protection in your fertility rituals.

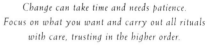

Change can take time and needs patience. Focus on what you want and carry out all rituals with care, trusting in the higher order.

the power of your thought that counts. You'll find that the more focused you are, the more likely you are to succeed. Of course, if something is preventing you physically from conceiving, then no amount of magic is going to overcome this. But miracles do happen, so follow your heart and take special care of yourself.

EMBRACING THE AGING PROCESS

I have read lots of false claims about aging, not just in magic spells but also in glossy magazines containing the latest miracle cures from the cosmetics industry. The unequivocal truth about the

Allegory of Eternity (*Peter Paul Rubens*).
We need not fear growing old. Discovering our
unique, spiritual selves and gaining insight
into an eternal future is the wonderful gift that
comes with aging.

aging process is that it cannot be stopped and nor should it be. It is part of our life experience, and an extremely vital part too. As each of us goes through the aging process, we learn to accept ourselves as we are and, more importantly, to use the wisdom that has come with experience. There are very few people who would really want to turn the clock back again to those dizzy days of teenage confusion. If you have a problem with your self-esteem because you have crossed the great watershed of middle age, treat this as the perfect opportunity to enter into your healing. Learn to be proud of yourself, no matter how old you are. Many people find extraordinary strengths and abilities as they enter into advanced years, and though the physical aging process is, without question, very challenging to all who meet it, it also provides enormous gifts totally unequated with youth.

As we age, we turn inward to seek our spiritual dynamic because in maturity we simply cannot compete with the outer face of youth. Of course, taking pride in one's appearance is very important no matter how old you are. There are all manner of herbal remedies available that can help to tone your skin naturally, and put a sparkle in your eye, and the most vital component for a healthy long life is diet. But to be deluded into thinking that anything can stop this aging process is ridiculous. You can of course enter into complete denial and undergo cosmetic surgery, but this simply cannot cut off, lift up, suck out, or nip and tuck who we are inside. The most effective antiaging agent I know of is a peaceful, loving heart. Those who have come to terms with themselves and their own mortality, and who selflessly live each day making life a better place to be for

Her Eyes are with Her Thoughts and They are Far Away *(Sir Lawrence Alma-Tadema).*
Inner strength and wisdom await us as we accept the lessons given to us in our lives.

everyone with whom they come into contact will be forever young in spirit.

So embrace the crone. She is the wise woman within each and every one of us, who has the ability to cut away lies and deceit until the truth lies naked and exposed. The crone no longer yearns for the unobtainable romanticism and ideology of youth; her power is that of the grandmother, fed and nurtured by her life's experiences. It comes from deep within her soul and it is without remission. The following ritual will enable you to meet this part of yourself.

During a full moon, light a white candle and some of your favorite incense and close your eyes. When you feel ready, call upon the energy of the moon to take you deep into yourself—to that special place that is yours and yours alone. Now

The Enamelled Chain (*Frank Markham Skipworth*). *We all have to leave our youth behind; aging is an essential progression in our life experience.*

call your grandmother crone energy and see her image appear in your mind's eye. Witness her power and the gifts she has to offer as you see yourself leaving your youth behind. Open your heart to release the pain and rage of aging, and know that you are loved by this grandmother crone. She is here to receive you as soon as you surrender into her arms. When you feel complete, take her into your heart. Leave the candle to burn down to the wick in homage to her.

Repeat this meditation as often as you wish, but specially during moments of doubt that we all encounter during our journey into later years.

CALLING IN ABUNDANCE

Abundance spells should be conducted on either a Monday or Thursday night during the waxing phase of the moon. Create your altar and decorate it with two vases full of yellow and orange flowers. These colors represent financial power. Entwine your gold and silver jewelry with the flowers and put at their base any other items that represent abundance to you. You also need to plait a green and orange cord together and knot it eight times. Arrange this into the shape of a sideways figure eight, the symbol of eternity, and place one vase in each circle. Place four green candles on the four directions and an orange candle in the center of the sacred circle. Light some incense made from sage (Mediterranean sage is particularly potent) and cinnamon. Score your name three times, together with the runic prosperity symbol (see page 85), in the wax of the orange candle, and anoint it with eight drops of mint oil.

Now all the preparations have been made, light the four directional candles, calling in the delvic realms as you do so. Evoke the power of the Goddess, light your orange candle and present it to each of the four corners while reciting the following incantation:

> *I call upon the spirits of air*
> *To send me wealth from the east.*
> *I call upon the spirits of fire*
> *To send me wealth from the south.*
> *I call upon the spirits of water*
> *To send me the wealth of the west .*
> *I call upon the spirits of earth*
> *To send me the wealth of the north.*
> *All is well. Blessed be.*

Now take time to write down exactly what you want, and even more importantly, why you want it. Should you be motivated by pure greed, be warned—you will run into trouble because the universe will deliver it straight back to your door. However, if you are seeking money or prosperity for an important reason which will truly improve your life and therefore that of others, the magic will undoubtedly provide everything you desire.

Lilium Bulbiferum or Fire Lily *(P.J. Redoute).*
Many spells include flowers to enhance the ritual.
Decorate your altar accordingly.

When you feel complete, extinguish the candles (remember, you should not blow them out), and repeat this process for the next three, five, or nine nights.

On the final night, call on the power of the Goddess to bless and protect the abundance you are now drawing toward you. Burn your paper in the orange flame and allow the rest of the candles to burn down completely. Scatter the flowers and ash onto the earth at the base of an elder or poplar tree. Both these trees resonate to the power of wealth and riches. Give thanks to the Goddess and to the spirit of the trees, and ask them to watch over your financial affairs. Take eight leaves from the tree, walk away without a backward glance, and place the leaves safely into a special bag that is decorated with prosperity symbols, which you should keep in your abundance corner—the far left-hand corner of your house in relation to the front door. Abundance and prosperity can come in all sorts of different shapes and sizes, so do not limit yourself to thinking just in terms of money. As I have said before, the universe sometimes has a very perverse sense of humor.

PURIFICATION RITUALS

If you need to cleanse an item you wish to use in a magical ritual, the best way is to hold it under fresh running water while calling on the Goddess to bless it. You can also immerse it into salted water. The salt is a very powerful cleanser. Leave the immersed item outside or on a window ledge for three days and nights during the waxing phase of the moon. This is particularly effective for crystals. However, if either of these methods are not practical, you can hold a special purification ceremony in which you present the item to each of the four corners. You can recite an incantation such as the following:

I call upon the sylphs of the
air to bless this.......[name of item].
I call upon the salamanders
of the south to bless this.......
I call upon the undines of the
west to bless this.......
I call upon the gnomes of the
north to bless this......
I present this.......to the
Goddess for her benediction.

This item is now ready to be used.

PERSONAL PURIFICATION RITUAL

Should you wish to perform a personal purification ceremony, you will need to find some birch twigs, which are traditionally used in cleansing rituals. This is a lovely ritual for the beginning of a completely new phase in your life or when you feel that you need to say goodbye to an

For a fresh start, gather twigs from the birch tree for your own purification ceremony. Lay them on your altar and use bunches of birch to symbolically exorcise your negative past.

A Wood Nymph *(Robert Poetzelberger)*. *Attract abundance into your life. Call on the power of the Goddess of prosperity and scatter your burnt offering beneath an elder or poplar tree.*

Life on the Banks of the Nile *(Roman mosaic). There is nothing new or strange about working with the universal energies. For the ancient Egyptians, symbols and rituals were an essential part of life.*

old part of yourself that no longer serves you. Trust your instinct about the appropriate day to do it. Our inner force is a powerful guide to find the "right time and place."

Throw away any clothes or items that are attached to this old way of life. You can ceremonially burn them if this feels appropriate. Clean out your cupboards, clear away old newspapers, letters and so on, and then make a list of what you wish to cleanse from your life.

Gather some birch twigs and decorate your altar with them. Birch twigs have been used in

purification and protection ceremonies for many thousands of years. Indeed, this is the origin of the idea that we use the birch to beat out any unclean thoughts.

Take time to draw a luxurious bath and add seven drops of juniper and rosemary oils. Bathe yourself thoroughly and celebrate that which you

Scene of Amorini (Roman fresco). Incorporate symbolic objects into your ritual work that feel right for you—flowers, shells, precious stones—and remember to give thanks to the Goddess.

which you wish to release. Dress in a loose-fitting robe and cast your sacred circle. Place 13 white candles around the perimeter and light some frankincense and myrrh incense. Enter by the east door of the circle, take a bunch of birch twigs and gently begin to slap the sides of your neck (do remember this is not an excuse to beat yourself up!). As you do so, say an incantation along the following lines:

I purify myself from old negative patterns,
I purify myself from the past,
I purify myself from loneliness and guilt.
May the spirit of the birch feed my soul.
All is well. Blessed be.

Now with the birth twigs work down your body to your solar plexus and repeat the incantation. Then work down to the soles of your feet. Once you feel complete, take a Native American sage stick (which can be bought in a wide variety of stores) and now "smudge" yourself

Magic practices can also benefit our pets, other animals, and the planet as a whole. Incorporate a photograph of your pet and the color brown into your healing ritual.

thoroughly with the smoke. You can also smudge all the rooms in the house if this feels appropriate to your ritual. When you are done, throw the birch twigs into a fire and watch them burn away your old life, and then add your list to the flame and watch this burn.

If it is safe, allow the 13 candles to burn down completely. If not, take one of the candles and place it in a safe place to burn undisturbed after you have extinguished the others. Light a white candle on each of the following 12 evenings (making 13 in all). As you light the candle recite your incantation and visualize your new life taking shape. On the final night, give thanks to the Goddess and decorate your altar with fresh birch twigs. After conducting this ceremony, your life will undoubtedly change. Just be open to receive what is for your highest good.

You can do this to release yourself from all sorts of negative habits—overeating, smoking, chewing your nails, and so on. The main thing is to be gentle and patient with yourself. You may have to repeat the ritual every month until you have broken the link with your addiction. Do keep at it, and very soon you should find that all will indeed be well. However, if you feel that you do need extra help, don't be afraid to seek professional counseling. Many of us find we need this at some stage of our lives, when we hit a particularly low spot. However, ritual work feeds your inner strength and resolve, and you will find this is a perfect complement to other forms of support and healing.

Twilight Fantasies *(Edward Robert Hughes). Practice the art of letting go through meditation—the journey to the inner self can give amazing glimpses of another dimension to our existence.*

CHAPTER 14

RITES OF PASSAGE

King Arthur and his Queen *(French book illustration). A pagan wedding, or hand-fasting is a wonderful way to proclaim your commitment to each other.*

HAND-FASTING CEREMONY

If you are one of the growing number of people who want to hold a wedding cele-bration that is not tied to any of the established religions, you may want to consider a pagan hand-fasting. This can be done during or after a civil ceremony, or merely conducted as a statement of commitment with your beloved.

Most pagan ceremonies are conducted outside because of the joy of being at one with the elements. It is also very powerful and wonderful to build a symbolic beltaine bonfire around which all the guests can dance, and reinstate their own marriage vows if they wish, after the ceremony. However, this ceremony can be just as easily adapted for an indoor ritual, suitable for both heterosexual and homosexual relationships and for couples from all religious backgrounds. The Crafts of the Wise apply to any creed, nation-ality, or sexual persuasion.

Before the day, the couple are required to buy two chalices to represent the great mysteries of love, pleasure, and emotion. These should be engraved with the date of the hand-fasting. Traditionally, the couple should wear two garlands of flowers, made from a combination of roses, gardenias, daisies, jasmine, and orchids on their heads or around their necks. It is a matter of personal choice whether the couple exchange rings but if they do, the rings should be made from white gold or silver to represent the Goddess. The couple select two supporters (the equivalent of a bridesmaid and a best man) who help them to prepare for the festivities.

The color of clothing worn at a hand-fasting is optional. However, many people like to marry in white or cream because it is symbolic of new beginnings. In very traditional pagan cere-monies, most don special robes, carrying a sword and staff, or they may be completely sky-clad!

Holding a wedding ceremony outdoors allows you to be at one with nature.

A pagan hand-fasting is a simple, natural, and joyful celebration of love without the involvement of any established religion. A bonfire, dancing, engraved chalices, and garlands of flowers are traditional features of the festivies.

Time, Death, and Judgement (*Cecil Schott*). *The hand-fasted couple make their own special vows. They may promise to stay together for life or for "as long as love shall last."*

The evening before the ritual, the two lovers, either separately or together, write down the vows they wish to say to each other. These need to be personal and to have special meaning for the couple. Some are happy to make life-long vows; others to make vows that will last "as long as love shall last." It is an especially beautiful gesture to light a large white or silver candle in honor of the Goddess and let it burn all through the night.

The morning before, the area is thoroughly cleansed by the two supporters using a besom, which is then blessed and laid on the floor before the altar facing east. The altar and the floor where the couple are to walk are strewn with masses of rosemary sprigs. The aroma that is released by walking on them is absolutely enchanting. Rosemary is said to evoke the souls of the ancestors and the Old Ones—just who you need to heap blessings upon you! If the ceremony is outside, the two supporters build a fire that is small enough for the couple to leap if they so wish. The altar is decorated with the seven chakra candles; in front of each is a vase of corresponding colored flowers. Leaves and branches from the myrtle, rowan, oak, and willow can be put around the edge of the altar. Myrtle is known as the love tree that keeps love alive and exciting, and preserves it. Rowan brings success and luck. Oak resonates to fertility and potency. Willow is the tree of moon magic and protection.

The hand-fasting ceremony is generally quite short and to the point; therefore, the guests usually stand in a circle around the couple, symbolizing the sacredness of life itself. The officiating priestess or priest welcomes the pair, who walk together into the circle from the east carrying their garlands of flowers and chalices filled with blessed water, wine, or champagne. They place the chalices on the altar. The Goddess is evoked, together with the four directions and their devic entities. The couple then speak their vows for all to hear, and once they are finished they offer the paper the vows are written on to the candle flame. The smoke takes these vows spiraling up to the seat of the gods and goddesses who preside over their destiny. The priest or priestess symbolically binds the couple hand-in-hand with a silk scarf. Finally, the couple exchange the garlands of flowers as an act of homage and respect for each other. This is also the perfect moment to exchange rings. Some traditions include an exchange of food and drink between the two, symbolizing abundance and prosperity. When all is complete, the couple jump the besom facing east— the direction of new beginnings. As soon as their feet touch the ground, their future begins together. They offer each other their chalices to drink from and the festivities begin.

The pair can also jump over the fire or dance around it to symbolize their fire and passion. The fire is then built up and everyone is encouraged to dance and sing. No union is complete without a huge feast and a lot of raucous music to make it a day to be remembered.

Your wedding day is special to you both, so do make it as personal as you can, and remember to choose what works for you. To stand as a couple before the Goddess, surrounded by nature and witnessed by a group of friends is not only deeply significant and moving but also a deeply intimate gesture of love and trust between the two of you. Do not take your vows lightly: it is well worth thinking about re-stating your

Love changes as each partner changes and moves on. By repeating your vows on each anniversary of the hand-fasting, you can reinstate your commitment and strengthen the relationship.

Love's Passing (*Evelyn de Morgan*). Remember to include a branch from the myrtle tree at the hand-fasting to keep love alive and exciting, rowan for success, and oak for fertility.

commitment every year on your anniversary in order to focus on the direction you are going in, both as individuals and as a couple.

NAMING AND BLESSING A NEWBORN

A variation of this tradition has been practiced for thousands of years by pagans and tribespeople from all over the world. Many traditions believe that the soul chooses the parents through which it incarnates because of the karmic lessons it needs to learn or to redress from a past incarnation. When the baby arrives in the world it is still closely linked to the world of spirits and, has inherent psychic qualities and ancient wisdom. Usually, as the child travels through its young life, these gifts become overshadowed or even obliterated by the behavior, attitudes, and expectations of the adults who surround it. Unless the link with the Divine is encouraged by parents and teachers, the child loses the memory of being a part of the oneness of all things, and it is lost completely. The struggle to remember this can be a life-long pursuit.

Allegory of Married Life depicting the Gods Vesta, Hymen, Mars, and Venus *(Alessandro Varotari, detail). A baby's psychic understanding is soon lost. Spiritual wisdom requires a return to that early awareness.*

The sacred custom of choosing a name has also been lost. Names are vibrations—special magical sounds that symbolically express the personality of the child. It is the Native American custom not to name a child until it begins to reveal its special personal characteristics, or until it has made a powerful statement about itself. The name can also be received as a vision or dream by the parent or by one of the wise elders. Names such as Light of Moon, Running Deer, and Sun Bear are, quite simply, soul-stirring.

In many ancient cultures the child would be given two names. The first was used to divert the evil eye and to protect the child from harm until adulthood, thus acting as a foil. The second name was secret and used only by intimate family members and guardians up until the time of puberty. This secret name would be spoken for the first time during a public naming ceremony in acknowledgment that the soul had changed its vibration into its first adult expression and was therefore ready to take responsibility for the full power of its name.

The custom of giving two names to a baby is still very popular; however, it is rare to find a parent who embraces the old teachings, or indeed understands their significance. Nevertheless, everyone's name, no matter how mundane, has a hidden meaning. For instance, my own name, Susan, is taken from the Hebrew for lily, meaning "full of grace." Those who are given this name take on the responsibility of shedding new light, grace, and purity wherever they tread. My sons are named Timothy and Matthew. Timothy means "honoring God." Those who bear the name need to learn the process of spiritual alchemy, the transmutation of fire and water into steam. Matthew means "gift of the lord." Those who have this name bring a gift to all they touch. There are books available (see Further Reading) that provide a comprehensive list of sacred names and their meanings. It is well worth investigating names to make sure you give your child the "occult" vibration you wish for him or her.

It is best to choose the time for your infant's blessing and naming ceremony to synchronize with the phase of the full moon. Traditionally this would be on the first day of full moon, that is the day *before* the full moon. It is especially auspicious to conduct the blessing when the full moon is passing through the child's astrological house of the moon, or as it makes a positive aspect with the ascendant or midheaven. I recommend that you consult a qualified astrologer to draw up a

natal chart for your child as soon as possible. This will help you to see what strengths and creative abilities should be encouraged in your child, as well as the challenges and weaknesses that will require patience, understanding, help, and guidance.

Traditionally, naming ceremonies are conducted outside in the light of the moon, thereby making the symbolic connection between the innocence of new life and the purity of nature. Choose an old tree such as an oak or beech under which to gather with friends and relatives. If you are conducting the ritual inside, use a small branch to symbolize the tree, but remember to honor the tree in its entirely before you take branches from it. Trees are the great "standing people," the gateway between heaven and earth, and the providers and shelters for the animal and plant kingdoms. Honor the spirit of the tree, then when you feel ready, set up an altar and decorate it with an abundance of sweet-smelling flowers. Place three bowls, preferably silver, on the altar. The first should contain a handful of grain, the second a handful of salt, and the third some blessed pure water. It is usual for the child's guardians or godparents to open the circle by walking around the group in a clockwise direction (called *deosil*) while they burn incense such as sage or frankincense to cleanse the space. The group may wish to chant while this is happening, or to sing appropriate songs. The parents or guardians evoke the protection of the four directions, together with the benediction of the Goddess, and lay the baby on the ground on a white cloth.

The guardians welcome the soul of the newly born in the name of the Goddess, and as they do so, they encircle the infant with the grain to ensure that the baby will never go hungry. They then encircle it with salt to symbolize purity, protection, and wisdom, and finally they make a circle of the blessed pure water to symbolize love, health, and happiness. At this stage in the ritual, the baby is now ready to be presented to the four directions, starting with the south, the place of innocence. At each direction, the baby's public and secret name are declared and bless-

ings for each are evoked. It is also declared that from this day until puberty, the secret name will never again be uttered in public at any time, or for any reason.

Finally, the baby is held aloft toward the moon for the blessings of the Goddess. The naming and blessing ceremony is now complete, and it is time for the guests to celebrate the life and future of this new addition to the human race.

The Dance of the Nymphs (*Jean Baptiste Camille Corot*). *The new baby's naming ceremony is traditionally held outside by moonlight, with an altar set up beneath a large, old tree.*

The Magic Garden, with Allegorical Figures of Courtesy, Love, Beauty, and Liberality (*from the* Roman de la Rose). *Magic will work best when carried out with love and a sincere wish for the highest good.*

DRAWING DOWN
THE BRIDGE OF SWORDS

When death comes to anyone we know, it inevitably affects us deeply. We are reminded that death is the ultimate, universal journey, from which there is absolutely no escape.

Sometimes death comes at the end of a long life, or after a lengthy debilitating illness; in these cases friends and family may feel a sense of blessed relief despite the loss. However, when death comes unexpectedly to take a life that on the surface appears to have much to live for, it is deeply traumatic for all concerned. We never seem prepared for the shock that accompanies sudden and unexpected death, and usually we are left feeling helpless and often guilt-ridden because of unresolved issues in relation to the one who has died. Our own mortality becomes sharply defined, and suddenly life seems all too fragile and short.

While it is most important to allow the mourning process to happen in its own time and pace, you may find that a simple ritual can play a very powerful part in helping to get through the natural state of mourning and to let go of the one who has died. Letting go can be especially difficult when death is unexpected or when mourning the death of a child.

The ritual should take place in a location where you feel safe to do your mourning. Sometimes people need to visit the house of the person who has died to say their farewells. Others feel they need to be out in the open, close to nature. Some need to gather together to help each other through the trauma; others need to be alone. Wherever you are and whoever you are with, set up a sacred altar. Decorate it with fresh wild flowers if possible. Create a sacred circle out of 13 stones or crystals on the altar, and place photographs or the name of the person in its center. Light a single white candle and burn a mixture of frankincense, myrrh, and fresh rosemary every day until you begin to feel able to find your center again. The tears are part of the process of cleansing and letting go, so do not be afraid to let them flow. Sometimes the tears flow for a long, long time. Should you feel that there are unresolved issues to attend to (for instance, you may have regrets over something that happened between you) write down these concerns or regrets on a piece of paper and place it underneath the photograph or name of the person. Leave them there until you feel it is the right time to deal with them—there is no rush. Light a candle and some incense and take the unresolved concerns from the altar. Now close your eyes, and recollect in your mind's eye the person you have lost. This can bring up very deep

Anubis, the Jackal-Headed God of the Dead and the God of Embalmers *(Egyptian wall painting). The Egyptians prepared their dead with great care in readiness for the journey to come.*

Say what you wish you had resolved while the person was alive and then watch what happens between the two of you. Take your time. This is an acutely holy moment in which extremely powerful experiences and realizations can occur. Allow yourself to receive and as you do so, you may well start to feel moments of intense freedom from deep within your soul. Breathe slowly, continuing to release the pain of loss from your body. Sometimes intense feelings of rage can also surface. Do not deny these feelings. Know that all is well and a great healing is taking place. Now in your mind's eye, draw down the bridge of swords—the link between the two worlds—and watch your friend take leave of you. See the Old Ones waiting to receive and help the dead one across. Know that all is well and things are exactly how they are meant to be. Once you feel you are complete, burn your unresolved issues in the candle flame and then scatter them onto the ground at the base of a tree.

You can repeat this ritual as often as you feel it is necessary. It is particularly healing to make some sort of ceremony on special days and anniversaries associated with the person.

emotions, so hug a pillow to your body and allow your feelings to flow. Breathe deeply to release your sorrow and if the tears flow, consider them to be both cleansing and healing at the same time. Once you feel that you are ready to continue, imagine placing your hand on the heart of the person and allow the person to place his or her hand on your heart. Feel the energy flowing between you. As soon as you feel able to continue, speak your truth to him or her either out loud or in your mind.

The death of someone we know can provide an opportunity for growth, forgiveness, and compassion because, though it is a time for mourning, it is also a time to honor and rejoice in the process of life. Those who embrace the Old Ways pay particular homage to death and reincarnation. Death signifies that a great karmic completion has taken place. The soul no longer needs its body to continue this particular cycle of growth. The evolution of the soul means that life cannot exist without death, any more than death can exist without life. This is the natural way of all things that is reflected back to us throughout our lives by the passing of the day into night, weeks into months, and months into years. The cycle of life and death is as inevitable as the seasons. Therefore nature also plays an important role in a death ritual.

Spiritual beliefs are most important at this time, and it is out of respect to the dead that their beliefs are taken into consideration. The "drawing down of the bridge of swords" is a death ritual using the Old Ways, but it can be incorporated into any traditional religious service, or used on its own.

PAGAN BURIALS

When someone who embraced the Old Ways dies, whether expectedly or unexpectedly, certain practical arrangements need to be made as soon as possible. It is very important to notify the undertaker of the person's particular pagan

Elaine from *La Mort D'Arthur* (*Charles Edwin Fripp*). *It is natural to grieve for the dead. But we also need to remember that all is well—death signifies a great karmic completion.*

beliefs, and to make sure that any religious icons, such as crucifixes, that run counter to the person's religious beliefs are removed from the chapel of rest. Most hospitals and undertakers nowadays are very sympathetic to these requests. You may need to find a suitable burial site that is not affiliated to any traditional religious beliefs. Consecrated cemeteries are not in accordance with paganism. But nowadays most cemeteries will have a special area set aside for the graves of those who wish to be buried on truly

Arbor Tristis: The Tree of Sorrow (from Durante's Herbario Nuovo). *This tree blooms only at night, its fragrant flowers shrinking away from the morning sun and the branches looking withered and dead.*

hallowed land. White flowers such as lilies are usually placed close to the coffin because they represent purity and new beginnings. Apples can be placed into the coffin since they are the pagan's symbol for the soul and provide sustenance for the deceased on the journey through the veil of darkness. A single green candle is placed in the direction of the west to signify that the dead are in a dream state, and in time they will reawaken in the east, just as the sun rises each morning in the east. Incense of rosemary and frankincense is burnt to call in the spirit of the ancestors so that they can care for this "newly born" soul before its journey to the other side. A candle is kept continually burning from the moment of death to the moment of final resting.

In ancient times, it was considered most important to dress the deceased in clothes that befitted their rank during life and to place personal possessions into the coffin. This custom stemmed from the belief that the dead carried on the spiritual journey to higher planes and would need these artefacts to sustain them. However, most modern pagans believe that once the soul has left it, the body is only an empty shell. So whatever is placed in the coffin or clothing the body is very much down to the personal discretion of friends and family. If possible, the house of the dead person should be cleansed and purified before the body is put to final rest (see page 146). Again, a combination of frankincense and rosemary is burnt in release the spirit, and a candle is burnt in a vigil of peace and serenity.

Death and the Indian (Stephen Baghot de la Bere). Early cultures knew the importance of properly mourning the dead. This is a process which cannot be hurried and should never be suppressed.

Juliet and her Nurse (*John Roddam Spencer-Stanhope*). *The deep sense of sadness we feel when a loved one dies is one of the sharpest pains most people will experience.*

The service should always be organized at the discretion of family and friends. Some pagans construct a funeral wreath of an inverted pentacle (white on black) and strew the altar with sprigs of rosemary. Two white candles burn on the altar as a symbol of the Goddess. Special words and quotations are read, and favorite songs are sung.

Should this be a burial ritual, the coffin is accompanied to its grave by four torch bearers representing the four directions. One walks in front, one at the rear, and one on each side of the coffin. The priest or priestess leads the way, carrying three boughs of evergreen, representing the triple face of the Goddess and everlasting life. At the site of the burial place, the four directions are evoked along with the power of the Old Ones. As the coffin is lowered into the ground, the priest or priestess raises their hand to the heavens and calls down the bridge of swords so that the soul can be transported to the other side with the help of the Old Ones.

Trees are a powerful link between heaven and earth. A tree planted in memory of the deceased will always be a precious reminder of the one who has moved on.

A handful of soil is thrown by the priest or priestess onto the coffin together with sprigs of rosemary and essence of frankincense. Friends and family may throw a handful of soil upon the coffin to say their last farewell. Thanks for the life of the person is offered to the God and Goddess and then the grave is covered with soil by hand-shovel, never by machinery. Finally, the four torches are placed at the four corners of the grave and left to burn out.

Once the ceremony has taken place, the mourners are encouraged to honor the life of their friend through festive celebration, safe in the knowledge that once they have completed the necessary lessons in the afterlife, they will return again into mortality. Although this may be difficult, it also helps the grieving process, giving everyone a chance to talk about their memories of the person who has passed on.

Many pagans plant a tree in memory of their loved ones, either near the grave or in some

The Storm Spirits (*Evelyn de Morgan*). *When someone dies, we need to call on the spirits of the ancestors to care for the newly transformed soul on its journey.*

The Angel of Death *(Evelyn de Morgan). Though we can never be prepared for the news that someone dear to us has died, we can continue to send them the transcending power of love.*

special sacred spot. This is a beautiful act, and somehow the tree takes on an extraordinary presence, as if it knows it represents a very special life. You can also do this if the body has been cremated. The ashes, and perhaps stones and crystals, are scattered into the hole into which the tree is then planted.

During your time of mourning it is important that you know that when someone you dearly love dies, life will never be quite the same again. The feeling of loss that you experience is often very difficult to come to terms with. However,

in the fullness of time you will find that the pain does turn into a much more gentle acceptance. With acceptance comes the understanding that, though something precious has been taken away, something very special has come to take its place. It may take years to come to this realization, but this is the deepest healing of the heart.

Life is never the same again after a death. But in time, we can come to a new awareness of life's mystery and magic, of which we are all a part.

Orpheus at the Tomb of Eurydice (*Gustave Moreau*). *Mourning can take many months or years, because love itself does not die. Repeat the ritual of the Bridge of Swords as often as you need to.*

FURTHER READING

AN ABC OF WITCHCRAFT by Doreen Valiente
(*Bookpeople, 1988*)

THE ALCHEMIST by Paulo Coelho
(*Harper San Francisco, 1995*)

THE ART OF SEXUAL ECSTASY by Margo Anand
(*Tarcher/Putnam, 1991*)

THE BOOK OF RUNES by Ralph Blum
(*St. Martin's Press, 1993*)

THE BOOK OF SIGNS by Rudolph Koch
(*Dover Publications, 1985*)

THE CELTIC LUNAR ZODIAC by Helena Paterson
(*Charles E. Tuttle Co., 1992*)

THE CELTIC TRADITION by Caitlin Matthews
(*Element, 1997*)

THE COMPLETE BOOK OF SAXON WITCHCRAFT
by Raymond Buckland (*Samuel Wiesner, 1974*)

THE COMPLETE BOOK OF TAROT by Juliette
Sharman-Burke (*St. Martin's Press, 1996*)

CUNNINGHAM'S ENCYCLOPEDIA
OF MAGICAL HERBS by Scott Cunningham
(*Llewellyn Publications, 1985*)

EARTH POWER by Scott Cunningham
(*Llewellyn Publications, 1987*)

ENTERING THE CIRCLE by Olga Kharitidi
(*Harper San Francisco, 1997*)

EVOCATION OF SPIRITS by Donald Michael Kraig
(*Llewellyn's Vanguard Series, 1995*)

GOOD MAGIC by Marina Medici (*Fireside, 1992*)

THE GRANDMOTHER OF TIME
by Zsuzsanna E. Budapest (*Harper San Francisco, 1989*)

THE GREAT SECRET by Eliphas Levi
(*Samuel Weisner, 1975*)

HANDS ACROSS TIME by Judy Hall
(*Findhorn Press, 1997*)

THE HIRAM KEY by Christopher Knight and
Robert Lomas (*Element Books, 1997*)

ILLUMINATIONS OF HILDEGARD OF BINGEN
by Hildegard of Bingen with commentary by
Matthew Fox (*Bear & Co., 1985*)

MOON MAGIC by Dion Fortune
(*Samuel Weisner, 1979*)

NOTIONS AND POTIONS by Susan Bowes
(*Sterling Publications, 1997*)

THE PSYCHOLOGY OF RITUAL by Murrey Hope
(*Element Books, 1991*)

THE SACRED PROSTITUTE by Nancy
Qualls-Corbett (*Inner City Books, 1988*)

THE SACRED POWER IN YOUR NAME
by Ted Andrews (*Llewellyn Publications, 1990*)

SACRED SEXUALITY by Jane Lyle and A. T. Mann
(*Element Books, 1995*)

THE SPIRAL DANCE by Starhawk
(*Harper San Francisco, 1989*)

THE STARS AND THE CHAKRAS by Joan Hodgson
(*De Vorss & Co., 1990*)

THE TREE OF ECSTASY by Dolores Ashcroft-
Nowicki (*Thorsons, 1991*)

TREE WISDOM by Jacqueline Memory Paterson
(*Thorsons, 1997*)

WHO'S WHO IN MYTHOLOGY by Michael Senior
(*Oxford University Press, 1996*)

INDEX OF SPELLS

*Incorporate candles, oils, and symbols to make
your spells more powerful.*

INDEX

INDEX

ACKNOWLEDGMENTS

In loving memory of Pusscat, my beloved familiar, friend, healer and companion,
and to life at Danny Cottage.

With grateful thanks to Peter Bridgewater, Viv, and Nicola from Ivy Press. You made this so easy and
fun to do. To Aisha-Rose and Melody—words cannot express the debt I owe you both for being there
for me come hell or high water and for being such great house companions. To William Morris for
your patience explaining the complexity of the thirteenth moon and for your absolutely stunning
calendar. To Chris Farrah-Mills from the Fallen Angel, Lewes, for giving me so much of your time. To
Janet Planet, Ali, Lulie Harker, Bex, and Sally Eden for being such wonderful friends and mentors.
Finally, to Mother Meera who cleared out ancient cobwebs in my soul. And to all of you who wish to
reconnect with the power of the Goddess.

PICTURE CREDITS